around

WASHINGTON D.C.

with

KIDS

by Kathryn McKay

5th EDITION

FODOR'S TRAVEL PUBLICATIONS

New York * Toronto * London * Sydney * Auckland

www.fodors.com

Credits
Writer: Kathryn McKay

Editor: Paul Eisenberg
Editorial Production: Evangelos Vasilakis
Production/Manufacturing: Angela L. McLean

Design: Fabrizio La Rocca, *creative director;*
Tigist Getachew, *art director*
Cover Art and Design: Jessie Hartland
Flip Art and Illustration: Rico Lins, Keren Ora
Admoni/Rico Lins Studio

About the Writer

Writer Kathryn McKay covers a lot of ground but her favorite place to write about is her hometown, Washington, D.C. She travels frequently with her two children and their nine cousins.

Fodor's Around Washington, D.C., with Kids

Fifth Edition
ISBN 978-1-4000-1930-4
ISSN 1526-1980

An Important Tip and an Invitation

Although all prices, opening times, and other details in this book are based on information supplied to us at press time, changes occur all the time in the travel world, and Fodor's cannot accept responsibility for facts that become outdated or for inadvertent errors or omissions. So always confirm information when it matters, especially if you're making a detour to visit a specific place. Your experiences—positive and negative—matter to us. If we have missed or misstated something, please write to us. We follow up on all suggestions. Contact the Around Washington, D.C. with Kids editor at editors@fodors.com or c/o Fodor's at 1745 Broadway, New York, New York 10019.

Special Sales

This book is available for special discounts for bulk purchases for sales promotions or premiums. Special editions, including personalized covers, excerpts of existing books, and corporate imprints, can be created in large quantities for special needs. For more information, write to Special Markets/Premium Sales, 1745 Broadway, MD 6-2, New York, New York 10019, or e-mail specialmarkets@randomhouse.com.

COUNTDOWN TO GOOD TIMES

GET READY, GET SET!

What child wouldn't be excited to touch a moon rock, see Dorothy's ruby slippers, or cruise along the C&O Canal in a canal boat pulled by mules? Washington may seem like a place that's mainly for grown-ups and school trips. After all, running the government of a superpower is serious stuff. But the city of the White House and the Capitol is also home to the International Spy Museum, the National Museum of Natural History, and the National Zoo. History that seems dry and dusty in the classroom comes alive for children as they visit landmarks they've seen in movies and on TV, ride horses through the same park where presidents have ridden, and watch thousands of dollars roll off the presses at the Bureau of Engraving and Printing. A big plus in Washington is that most attractions are free.

GET PREPARED
You could just take the Metro to the Smithsonian stop, get off at the National Mall, and wander around. And you'd probably have fun.

Or you can prepare yourself and your children. Flip through this book. The first time, flip through fast, and check out Abe Lincoln and his admirers in the lower right corner. Next, take the time to read the listings, and use the directories in the back of the book to find just what you're looking for. Last but not least, bring this book with you as you explore. It'll help you get even more out of your visits.

Before you leave, call for information—especially if you go on a holiday (when Washington is generally very crowded). The hours listed in this book are the usual operating hours. Some places are open longer or shorter or not at all on holidays, and fees and hours are always subject to change. For those sights that do charge admission, we list only the regular adult, student (with ID), and kids' prices; children under the ages specified are free. In addition, some discounts are offered for families or for a particular status or affiliation; it never hurts to ask.

To find current kids' activities and events going on in and around the city, look in the "Weekend" section of Friday's *Washington Post* and in *Washington Parent,* a monthly publication available free at libraries and many grocery stores.

GET AROUND

For train lovers, riding Washington's Metro (subway) system can be as thrilling as exploring your destination. But before you go, remember that Metro stations don't have public restrooms. Buy your ticket at the Farecard machines, or better yet, let your kids put their math minds to work and put the money in the machines. The base fare is $1.35; the actual price you pay depends on the time of day and distance traveled. Children 4 and under ride free. But after you go through the turnstiles to enter, consider collecting your kids' cards. You'll need them again to exit.

Each line of the Metrorail is color coded: red, orange, blue, green, and yellow. You can move from one line to another at transfer stations. As a precaution, be sure shoelaces are tied and scarves are tucked in before you ride Metro escalators, some of which are more than 200 feet long. If your children are afraid of heights or you have a little one in a stroller, take the elevators. All the stations have them, though about a third of them are across the street from Metro entrances.

If, on the other hand, you decide to navigate behind the wheel, it's relatively easy to get your bearings in this diamond-shape city. With the Capitol as its hub, Washington is composed of four quadrants—Northwest (NW), Northeast (NE), Southwest (SW), and Southeast (SE)—divided by North, South, and East Capitol streets and, on the west side of the Capitol, by the National Mall instead of a street. Within each of these quadrants, the roads running north and south are numbered, and east to west roads are named after letters of the alphabet. (You won't find an A or B street because A Street became the Mall and East Capitol Street, and B Street was renamed Constitution Avenue to the north and Independence Avenue to the south.) After the lettered streets come longer street names in alphabetical order, and the alphabetical lineup repeats itself until the Maryland and Virginia borders. Add to the mix a number of diagonal avenues named for states, the most prominent being Massachusetts, Connecticut, and Pennsylvania avenues. Traffic circles and one-way streets can add to the confusion for adults but can be fun for kids, who can look for the statues and fountains in the centers of the circles.

Around the outskirts, the Capital Beltway girds Washington like—you guessed it—a big belt. If you do go downtown, keep in mind that parking may be limited and expensive, especially during the week. For most suburban sights, parking is free and plentiful.

GET ORIENTED

When you arrive at a sight, be prepared to walk through metal detectors and open your bags for security personnel. Visit the information desk for maps and brochures, and inquire about children's programs. Also, show your kids how to recognize staff or security people, and designate a time and place—some visible landmark—to meet in case you become separated. It goes without saying that you should keep an eye on your children at all times, especially if they are small.

GET GOING
Finally, after you've planned and scheduled and traveled, have fun. And try to be as spontaneous as your children.

GET IN TOUCH
We'd love to hear from you. What did you and your children think about the places we recommend? Have you found other places we should include? Send us your ideas via e-mail (c/o editors@fodors.com, specifying *Around Washington, D.C., with Kids* on the subject line) or snail mail (c/o Around Washington, D.C., with Kids, Fodor's Travel, 1745 Broadway, New York, NY 10019). In the meantime, get ready, get set, and go have a great time seeing Washington, D.C., with your kids!

KATHRYN MCKAY

ARLINGTON NATIONAL CEMETERY

A cemetery doesn't seem like a place for children, but this one, the most famous and most visited cemetery in the country, is different. Even the most cynical observer of Washington politics may find a lump in his throat or a tear in his eye while here, on top of which there's plenty here to see.

At the Tomb of the Unknowns, the resting place for unidentified fallen soldiers, soldiers from the Army's 3rd U.S. Infantry Regiment (Old Guard) keep watch 24/7, regardless of weather. Each sentinel marches 21 steps (children can count them silently), clicks his or her heels, and faces the tomb for 21 seconds, symbolizing the 21-gun salute—all while carrying an M-14 rifle weighing 10 pounds. The changing of the guard is a precise ceremony, held every half hour during the day from April through September and every hour the rest of the year. (At night, when the cemetery's closed, it's every two hours.)

MAKE THE MOST OF YOUR TIME You can reach Arlington on the Metro, by foot over Arlington Memorial Bridge (southwest of the Lincoln Memorial), or by car—there's a large parking lot by the visitor center on Memorial Drive. Also, the Tourmobile bus (*www.tourmobile.com*, tel. 202/554–7950) and Old Town Trolley (*www.oldtowntrolley.com*, tel. 202/832–9800) both have Arlington National Cemetery stops in their loops.

West end of Memorial Bridge, Arlington, VA.
Metro: Arlington National Cemetery

 Free; parking $1.25 per hr. Tourmobile $6, children 3–11 $3.50

 Apr–Sept, daily 8–7; Oct–Mar, daily 8–5

 703/607–8000; www.arlingtoncemetery.org

6 and up

Kids may also be interested in famous grave sites. More than 300,000 American war dead and many notable Americans are interred in these 624 acres. Even kids who don't yet know the name John F. Kennedy may find the eternal flame at his final resting place fascinating. He's buried near two of his children, who died in infancy, and his wife, Jacqueline Bouvier Kennedy Onassis. His is the most visited grave in the country. If the flame is extinguished by rain, wind, or any other cause, a continuously flashing electric spark reignites it. Nearby, a simple white cross marks the resting place of his brother Robert. Although William Howard Taft, 27th president and Supreme Court justice, lies here, as do famous veterans Joe Louis (boxer), and Abner Doubleday (reputed inventor of baseball), the sobering sea of marble tombstones in Section 60 may have the most present-day resonance: This is where those who served in Iraq and Afghanistan are buried.

If you like this sight you may also like the Washington National Cathedral (#5).

KEEP IN MIND

While at Arlington, you will probably hear the clear, doleful sound of a bugler playing taps or the sharp reports of a gun salute. On average, 27 funerals are held here daily. You'll want to remind your child that this is sacred ground; respect and quiet are always necessary.

EATS FOR KIDS No food or drink is allowed at the cemetery, but you can purchase and drink bottled water at the **Women in Military Service for America Memorial** near the entrance. **Whitlow's on Wilson** (2854 Wilson Blvd., tel. 703/276–9693) specializes in hamburgers, but your kids may be more interested in playing foosball. Your kids might not care that the pasta at **Faccia Luna** (2909 Wilson Blvd., tel. 703/276–3099) is homemade or that the pizza is baked on the hearth, but you might.

AUDUBON NATURALIST
SOCIETY'S WOODEND

Don't let bad weather keep the kids inside. In fact, no matter what it's like outside there'll be something interesting to see and do at this nature wonderland. Snow and mud make finding animal tracks easier as you play nature detective. On hot, humid days, crickets and cicadas form a chorus and butterflies dance in wildflower meadows. On cool, crisp fall days, you can see varied leaf colors reflected in the large pond. But on any day, you'll hear the trill of birdsong, because the Audubon Naturalist Society (ANS) has turned the grounds into a nature preserve.

A self-guided nature trail winds through this verdant 40 acres and around the local ANS's suburban Maryland headquarters. The estate is known as Woodend, as is the mansion, which was designed in the 1920s by Jefferson Memorial architect John Russell Pope. Allowing time to marvel at Mother Nature, you can complete the ¾-mile trail in about one hour. Parents of babies should use a carrier rather than a stroller, as most of the trail has wood chips. Along the nature trail, you'll see not only birdhouses and bird feeders, but also houses for flying squirrels.

KEEP IN MIND The beauty and peace of this sanctuary might be punctured from time to time by the sight of a Cooper's hawk making a meal out of a morning dove, the remains of a mouse that an owl discarded, or by the roar of the Washington Beltway.

EATS FOR KIDS You can pack a picnic for your Woodend adventure at nearby **Chevy Chase Supermarket** (8531 Connecticut Ave., tel. 301/656–5133), a neighborhood institution since 1958. Or about 3 miles west, in downtown Bethesda, you can nibble your way around the world at any of 180 restaurants. As its name implies, **Mama Lucia's** (4907 Cordell Ave., tel. 301/907–3399) specializes in Italian dishes. Monday is pasta special night; on Tuesday, pizza prices are slashed. Friendly, quick service and red chili-pepper lights swooping across the ceiling make **California Tortilla** (4862 Cordell Ave., tel. 301/654–8226) a favorite for families.

8940 Jones Mill Rd., Chevy Chase, MD

 301/652-9188;
www.audubonnaturalist.org

 Free; children's and family
programs starting at $10,
camps $110–$725

 Daily sunrise–sunset; bookshop
M–F 10–5, Sa 9–5, Su 12–5

 3–9 (camps for teens, too)

For a break from the outdoors (but not the heat—the mansion isn't air-conditioned), ask at the Woodend office if you can see the library. Along with books for adults, it contains hundreds of stuffed American birds. The mansion is rented for weddings, bar mitzvahs, and other celebrations, but it's generally open on weekdays 9–5.

During family programs (which include parents), classes, and one- to two-week camps, educated naturalists foster environmental awareness and unlock nature's mysteries. Each program focuses on a nature-oriented theme, such as flying squirrels, meadow habitats, pond life, or "metamorphosis magic," and includes such hands-on activities as catching insects, fishing for pond creatures with nets, or investigating rotting log communities. ANS fairs on the first Sunday in May attract thousands. While you shop at the crafts fair, your children can enjoy animal demonstrations and kiddie crafts.

If you like this sight you may also like Rock Creek Park (#19).

MAKE THE MOST OF YOUR TIME Wear old

clothes and apply your sunscreen and bug repellent before you arrive. If you're with a little one and want to be able to use your stroller, head down the driveway from the parking lot. When you reach the huge walnut tree, you're near what some kids call the "secret pond." Every stick, leaf, rock, and insect needs to stay at Woodend. If your little collectors are disappointed by this rule, you can visit the bookshop. It sells souvenirs for young naturalists, including nature books, puzzles, T-shirts, and games.

BOWIE BAYSOX BASEBALL

Minor-league baseball offers major-league fun for young fans of the Bowie Baysox, a Class AA Eastern League affiliate of the Baltimore Orioles. Not only can you see what's happening better at the 10,000-seat Prince George's Stadium than at 50,000-seat, major-league ballparks, but you'll find as much action off the field as there is on it.

As a Baysox player slides into base, your children can slip down the slide at their own play area on the concourse area in view of the first base line. As players circle the diamond, your kids can circle on a carousel, which runs during the entire game, except while the national anthem plays. Little hurlers test their throwing arms in pitch-speed games.

Meanwhile, young collectors can spread out their baseball card collections in the ample bleachers, and there's plenty of room for teenagers to move a few seats away and pretend they're not really with Mom or Dad. When the ballpark is crowded, fans get more boisterous, which is also part of the entertainment. Giveaways and games throughout the summer can

MAKE THE MOST OF YOUR TIME Two Class A minor-league
teams also play in Washington's outfield: the **Frederick Keys** (tel. 877/846–5397; www.frederickkeys.com) in Frederick County, Maryland, and the **Potomac Nationals** (tel. 703/590–2311; www.potomacnationals.com) in Prince William County, Virginia. The Bowie stadium is a little larger, and since the Baysox are Class AA, the quality of play is a little better. Otherwise the experience is similar. Based on where you live or where you're visiting, you may want to try one of the others.

Prince George's Stadium,
4101 N.E. Crain Hwy.
(U.S. 301), Bowie, MD

301/805–6000 information,
301/464–4865 tickets; www.baysox.com

Upper reserve seats $11
ages 13 and up, $9 children
12 and under; reserved
seats $14; 2 and under free
for all seats

 Early Apr–Labor Day

4 and up

yield such precious kid keepsakes as caps, jerseys, and mugs. On Saturday nights, holidays, and occasional weeknights, postgame fireworks light up the sky.

Of course, if your kids are actually interested in the game itself, they can keep track of it on electronic scoreboards and a large screen that shows replays from the field and fans in the stands. (So smile! You may be on camera.) And if your kids come wearing their youth athletic uniforms, they'll get in free Sunday through Thursday. All the activity makes minor-league baseball and children a natural double-play combination. The only real downside is that your family won't see today's superstar . . . but you might see tomorrow's!

If you like this sight you may also enjoy the Washington Nationals (#4).

KEEP IN MIND
For die-hard fans, it's easier to get autographs here than at major-league stadiums. Baysox officials recommend arriving an hour and a half before the game to catch players between warm-ups and game time. Several players move up to the majors each year, so you never know whose signature may end up being a treasure later.

EATS FOR KIDS At the **Kids' Stand,** peanut-butter sandwiches, juice, and such typical baseball fare as hot dogs cost $1 each. (Sorry, the Kids' Stand is just for kids!) Adults pay a little more at the concession stands but get more choices. You can eat pub-type fare while watching the game from the **Diamond View** restaurant, when it's open. On most weekends and some weekdays it's booked for parties.

BUREAU OF ENGRAVING AND PRINTING

65

Show me the money! It's here—some $637 million printed daily—and we defy you not to enjoy watching as bills roll off the presses. And despite the lack of free samples, the guided, 35-minute bureau tour is one of the city's most popular attractions.

The United States began printing paper currency in 1862 to finance the Civil War and because there was a coin shortage. Two men and four women separated and sealed by hand $1 and $2 U.S. notes printed by private companies. Today, the bureau employs approximately 2,500 people, who work out of two buildings: this one and one in Fort Worth, Texas.

On tour, your children can look through wide windows to see four steps in the money-making process. First, color is added to the paper. In the second section, both sides of the bills are printed in large 32-note sheets—back side first. (Bureau employees refer to bills as "notes.") Third, machines inspect the notes for defects. For example, if a sheet was folded instead of flat during the process, the notes may only be half printed. Rejects

EATS FOR KIDS There's something for everyone at the **U.S. Department of Agriculture Cafeteria** (12th and C Sts. SW, tel. 202/488–7279). Get visitor stickers at the front desk, then choose from seven food stations and a buffet. Choices include grilled cheese and hot hearty meals with veggies.

MAKE THE MOST OF YOUR TIME March–August, required same-day timed-entry tickets are issued starting at 8 at the Raoul Wallenberg Place SW ticket booth. Waits to get in can be up to two hours, and if a tour bus arrives as you do, you may be stuck outside longer. September–February is considered an off peak time, so tickets are not required and waits likely will not be as long. While waiting, examine some money with your kids and amuse them with some fun facts. For example: If you spent $1 every second, it would take 317 years to spend $10 billion; a mile-high stack of currency would contain over 14½ million notes.

14th and C Sts. SW. Metro: Smithsonian
(Independence Ave. exit)

 Free

 202/874-2330; www.moneyfactory.gov

M–F 9–10:45 and 12:30–2 Aug–May
also open 2–3:45 and 5–7; hrs subject
to change

6 and up

are shredded and sold or recycled. In the final area, serial numbers and Federal Reserve seals are printed, and the notes are cut.

Each $1 note costs 4¢–5.2¢ to print. Larger denominations cost a little extra because of security enhancements such as watermarks, color-shifting ink, and security threads. Hold one of these bills up to the light to see the vertically embedded threads. Environmentally minded kids will be glad to know that no trees are cut down to make paper currency; it's made of 75% cotton and 25% linen.

It may sound crazy to adults, but kids like to buy bags of shredded money in the bureau's gift shop. A small bag costing $2 contains $150 worth of bills that didn't pass inspection. Five bucks gets you a postcard that looks like currency, with your photo on it.

If you like this sight you may also like the National Gallery of Art and Sculpture Garden (#33).

KEEP IN MIND Would you like to make money? Ten-year-old Emma Brown did. She was the youngest employee in bureau history, but she didn't work here for the fun of it. Emma's brother, the family breadwinner, was killed in action during the Civil War, leaving Emma to care for her disabled mother and the rest of the family. Emma's congressman gave her a political appointment so she could make money by making money.

C&O CANAL NATIONAL
HISTORICAL PARK'S BOAT RIDES

When you hear the horn blow, boarding time is near. Your family can take a leisurely, mule-drawn boat ride through the lock, down the Chesapeake & Ohio (C&O) Canal, and back again. Although you won't go far physically—less than a mile—you can mentally travel all the way back to the 1800s as costumed guides teach you about canal life. Interestingly, the C&O goes to neither the Chesapeake nor the Ohio. The Baltimore & Ohio (B&O) Railroad beat the canal to the Ohio River, and the railroad's success eventually put the canal out of business. Ironically, construction of both the C&O and the B&O began on the same day, July 4, 1828. When canal construction ended in 1850, there were 74 lift locks stretching from downtown D.C. to Cumberland, Maryland. Nevertheless, for a time the canal did prove to be economical for traders moving goods, especially coal, to the port of Georgetown, from which ships traveled to the lower Chesapeake and the Atlantic Ocean.

Most children are fascinated by the canal boat's engines: four mules named Ada, Molly, Lil, and Nell take turns pulling the 12-foot-wide barge along the towpath. As the boat passes

MAKE THE MOST OF YOUR TIME Across M Street is the oldest building in Washington: the **Old Stone House** (3051 M St. NW, tel. 202/426–6851), built in 1764. Rooms are furnished with simple, sturdy artifacts of 18th-century life, but usually the best part for kids is the garden in back. Admission is free.

1057 Thomas Jefferson St. NW.
Metro: Foggy Bottom

 202/653–5190;
www.nps.gov/choh

 $7 ages 15 and up,
$5 children 4–14

Apr–Oct, W–Su 11, 1:30, and 3
(times may change; call ahead)

4 and up

under the 15-foot-wide bridge at Thomas Jefferson Street, it may only be a canal worker's foot keeping the boat from hitting the bridge.

Amid tales of canal life, the guides may treat you to some music and a few jokes. One example: "Along the canal, you may notice moss on the sides of the lock. Can you guess the name of the bird that uses the moss for its nest? The lock moss nester!" The rest of the ride should be all downhill.

If you like this sight you may also like Great Falls (#49). You'll get another look at the canal and another chance to see the mules.

KEEP IN MIND
Don't be alarmed if your guide jumps off the boat to help with the lines and puts a child in charge for a few minutes. Said child will probably take possession of the horn and may even wear a captain's hat to make sure passengers stay in line. Eventually the guide will come back and your little captain will go back to being a kid.

EATS FOR KIDS Drop anchor at **Washington Harbour** (3000 K St. NW, tel. 202/295–5000), a complex of condos, offices, and restaurants. Stroll the waterfront with ice cream from **Edy's Ice Cream** (tel. 202/298–8331). Try traditional chocolate or go for tropical sorbet. For a more substantial treat, munch on popcorn shrimp from **Tony and Joe's** (tel. 202/944–4545) while watching seagulls soar, looking for their own food.

THE CASTLE (SMITHSONIAN BUILDING)

I n London, castles may be for kings and queens, but here in Washington, the Castle is for us common folk who want to map out a day on the National Mall, a historic expanse of lawn between the Potomac River and Capital Reflecting Pool. Called the Castle because of its magnificent towers and turrets, this first Smithsonian building is a Norman-style structure made of red sandstone. Completed in 1855, it originally housed all of the Smithsonian's operations—hard to imagine now—including the science and art collections and research laboratories. It was even the home of the first secretary of the Smithsonian and his family.

In the 1890s American buffalo (aka bison) were kept in a pen behind the Castle. These once-numerous beasts had been hunted so relentlessly for decades that their numbers were dwindling. Determined to prevent their extinction, Samuel Pierpont Langley, the Smithsonian's third secretary, convinced Congress to provide a site where bison and other animals could be protected and displayed. This decision marked the beginning of the National Zoo.

MAKE THE MOST OF YOUR TIME Since the Castle opens an hour and a half before the other Mall museums, early risers can get a good jump on their adventures.

EATS FOR KIDS The following Mall museums have food courts (*see* each listing): the National Air and Space Museum (#39), National Gallery of Art and Sculpture Garden (#33), National Museum of American History (#30), National Museum of the American Indian (#29), and the National Museum of Natural History (#27).

1000 Jefferson Dr. SW. Metro: Smithsonian

 Free

Daily 8:30–5:30

 202/633–1000, 202/357–1729 TTY; www.si.edu

2 and up

Start at the Castle's Smithsonian Information Center, where you can learn all about the museum, education, and research complex—19 museums and galleries (10 of which are on the Mall) and a zoo—that is the Washington area's Smithsonian Institution. An 18-minute video overview plays constantly—if your kids will sit still that long, you may get to watch it. Better yet, talk to the very knowledgeable volunteers, or pick up a brochure. Touch-screen monitors at heights for both children and adults display information on visitor services. Interactive videos provide more detailed information on the museums as well as other attractions in the capital city. Push a button on the electronic map to locate Arlington National Cemetery or to light up the entire Metro system. A braille map of the city wasn't designed for children, but draws them nonetheless.

If you like this site you may also like the Smithsonian American Art Museum and the National Portrait Gallery (#15).

KEEP IN MIND You can't see the Smithsonian's entire collection of objects, artifacts, specimens, and creatures—137 million and growing, due to gifts, purchases, and, at the zoo, births—as only an estimated 1%–2% of the collections are on display, but unlike the stuff under kids' beds, objects are cataloged and used in research.

CHILDREN'S MUSEUM OF ROSE HILL
MANOR PARK

The first place kids go in this historic home is the same one they seek out in most houses: the playroom. However, the playroom of this Georgian home, the last residence of the first elected governor of Maryland, is full of replicas of toys and games from more than 100 years ago: corncob checkers, a dollhouse, a rocking horse, a tea set, dress-up clothes, and mechanical coin banks. Lift a lever on these banks to move a penny from a whale to a boat, a monkey to a box, or Uncle Sam's arm to a little black bag.

Costumed guides meet families in the playroom, and the antique adventure continues. Upstairs there's a master bedroom, domestic quarters, a study room, and a child's bedroom with Early American toys. A 1½-hour tour at most historical sights would be too long for kids, but guides here are experienced in showing children what life was like during our country's infancy. Along the way, they explain how fireplaces, bed warmers, and windows were used in different weather and how people lived without modern conveniences like plumbing. In addition, the tour includes numerous hands-on activities. Back downstairs, children can

MAKE THE MOST OF YOUR TIME Rose Hill Manor is well worth the 50-mi drive from D.C. Take Interstate 270 north to U.S. 15 at Frederick, exiting at Motter Avenue. Turn left on 14th Street and left on North Market Street. The entrance is just past the Governor Thomas Johnson High School.

1611 N. Market St. (Rte. 355), Frederick, MD

301/694–1650; www.rosehillmuseum.com

$5 adults, $4 children 3–17

Apr–Oct, M–Sa 10–4, Su 1–4; Nov, Sa 10–4, Su 1–4; Dec, hrs vary

5–12

card wool, operate a loom, add stitches to a quilt, or try out 19th-century cooking equipment. If the tour gets tiresome, escape to the gardens.

The tour itself continues outside to a one-room log cabin, a reminder that the majority of people in the early 1800s were not to the manor born. Most settlers lived in simple homesteads. In the blacksmith's shop, kids learn how 19th-century "smithies" spent most of their time repairing such ironwork as axes and chains. In the carriage museum, your children can find foot warmers in carriages and sleighs but they can't climb onto the exhibits. They can play in the Early American garden and orchard that contains more than 100 species of herbs, flowers, fruits, and vegetables. If you're interested, the last tour stop is the requisite museum store, which carries postcards and inexpensive trinkets.

If you like this sight you may also like the Sully Historic Site (#14).

KEEP IN MIND
During the Civil War Encampment in July, Union and Confederate soldiers march, fire cannons, and talk to kids about life in the 1800s. If military history isn't for you, consider the ice-cream festival in August.

EATS FOR KIDS You can pack your own lunch or purchase some crackers or candy in the museum store and spread out at picnic tables anytime. **Pretzel and Pizza Creations** (210 N. Market St., tel. 301/694–9299) puts a new twist on pretzels, whose 30 varieties include chocolate, peanut butter, and rainbow sprinkle. Children's books on shelves in the back and cups of cappuccino encourage kids and their parents to linger.

CLAUDE MOORE COLONIAL FARM
AT TURKEY RUN

Back in the 1770s, children didn't have to go to school, wear shoes, or take a nightly bath. Some modern children might even think those early days were easy—that is, until they visit this re-created Colonial farm. Here child volunteers portraying Colonial kids (when school is closed) explain that children couldn't go to school because they worked all day on the farm. Those who could fit into one of the few pairs of shoes a family might own were lucky, as they were less likely to suffer from sore feet. Frequent baths weren't considered healthful—nor were they practical, since heating enough water for a tub took a long time.

Even when the Colonial kids aren't here, you and your children can watch historical interpreters in period clothing demonstrate how a farming couple eked out a living by tending to tobacco and wheat fields, a vegetable garden, and farm animals.

MAKE THE MOST OF YOUR TIME Encourage your kids to go to the bathroom before you arrive. The farm is equipped with the modern-day equivalent of outhouses (the portable toilet).

EATS FOR KIDS If you packed a lunch, grab one of the picnic tables at the farm entrance. A few miles away, the **McLean Family Restaurant** (1321 Chain Bridge Rd., tel. 703/356–9883) has been serving Greek and American dishes for more than 35 years. At **Rocco's Italian Restaurant** (1357 Chain Bridge Rd., tel. 703/821–3736), child-size pizzas are best sellers, but those with more sophisticated palates can order manicotti, rigatoni, and ravioli. After eating, kids (and adults) can get a lollipop for the road.

6310 Georgetown Pike, McLean, VA

 703/442-7557; www.1771.org

 $3 ages 13 and up, $2 children 3–12; Market Fair $5 ages 13 and up, $2.50 children 3–12

 Apr–mid-Dec, W–Su 10–4:30

 2 and up

A dirt path winds around an orchard, fields, a tobacco barn, a pond, a hog pen, and an English-style, one-room farmhouse. The walk is comfortable, and a well-napped preschooler can make the trip handily. Pushing a stroller along the root-laden path is tricky, but possible.

During Market Fairs, held the third full weekends in May, July, and October, families enjoy making Colonial crafts (about $1 each), marching in parades, and watching puppet shows. And just as in the 1770s, you can eat and shop. Reproductions of 18th-century pottery, jewelry, fragrant soaps, clothing, and toys are for sale on Market Fair days, too.

By the end of the day, your kids will probably have discovered that Colonial life was indeed tough, but you'll have discovered that a trip to Claude Moore is easy.

If you like this sight you may also like the Discovery Creek Children's Museum (#56).

KEEP IN MIND When Colonial kids played, they either used their imaginations or made toys out of things that had no monetary value and weren't needed elsewhere. They made marbles out of clay and turned split sapling trees into hoops, which they rolled on the ground with a stick. Try rolling a hula hoop with a stick. It's harder than you might think.

COLLEGE PARK AVIATION
MUSEUM

Walk by the animatronic Wilbur Wright and he'll tell you about the thrills and chills of teaching pilots to fly in 1909. Children don't have to just take Wilbur's word for it: they'll see it for themselves at this interactive museum dedicated to early aviation.

Your children will be challenged and exhilarated as they turn and pull levers, knobs, and switches on flight simulators. They can try starting a plane's engine, not by turning a key as it's done today, but the way it was done before World War I, by turning a propeller. (Hint: Make sure no one is in the way and push down as hard as you can. Then step back. It's loud!) Your kids can even dress like pilots of yore, donning goggles, silk scarves, and helmets to pose for pictures against an airplane backdrop.

Also inside, a full-scale replica of the 1911 Wright B Aeroplane, a restored 1918 Curtiss Jenny, a 1932-era Monocoupe, and a Berliner Helicopter grace the largest gallery of this airy museum, which opened in 1998. If you notice a similarity to the National Air and

MAKE THE MOST OF YOUR TIME
For a list of what's happening on the day you visit, check the flight desk at the front of the museum. It may list "How Things Fly," of interest to older kids, or Peter Pan Club activities, such as making paper airplanes, for preschoolers. In addition, when Maryland or Prince George's County public schools are closed, the museum sponsors aviation craft activities. If you don't make your own souvenir, though, you may want to take home a flight of fancy from the museum's gift shop, which is full of aviation toys and games, many under $5.

1985 Cpl. Frank Scott Dr., College Park, MD.
Metro: College Park

301/864-6029;
www.collegeparkaviationmuseum.com

 $4 adults,
$2 children 2–18
and students

 Daily 10–5

2 and up

Space Museum, you're not imagining it; both museums were designed by the same architectural firm. But here you can see and do everything in an hour and you won't have to worry about losing your children in crowds. For an extra dollar, you can "pitch" and "roll" hand controls of the Wright Experience Flight Simulator to maneuver turns and gain altitude while flying over computerized 3-D images of historic College Park Airport (the world's oldest continually operating airport) as it appeared when the Wright Brothers were teaching the first military pilots to fly.

Outside there's more to see and do. Children ages 5 and under get a feel for flying by riding around in wooden planes on a mini-runway. Gaze out the museum's large glass wall onto College Park Airport.

If you like this site you may also like the National Air and Space Museum (#39).

KEEP IN MIND
Since the first edition of this book came out in 2000, this museum is the number one place that readers say they're happy to know about. Kids love it. It's best to drive, because the nearest Metro stop, College Park, is a significant walk from the museum (about 15 minutes), and since it's on the Green Line, it means a transfer for many people. Fortunately, parking is plentiful.

EATS FOR KIDS If your kids like to watch planes, bring lunch and eat on the museum balcony, overlooking the airport. Or follow the planes painted on a path outside to the aviation-theme **94th Air Squadron Restaurant** (5240 Paint Branch Pkwy., tel. 301/699–9400). The food used to be as iffy as airplane food but it's improved in recent years. Bring your receipt from the museum and you can receive 10% off. To take off for guaranteed good eats, try **Noodles** (7320 Baltimore Ave. [Route 1], tel. 301/779–5300), about 10 minutes away, where you can choose from oodles of noodles.

CORCORAN GALLERY OF ART

59

Create a flip book like the flip art in this book. Style your own fashion photo shoot. Turn everyday objects into works of art. These are some of the activities in store during family programs at one of the oldest U.S. museums.

During the Corcoran's Family Days, the museum becomes a family funfest. To celebrate those famous birthdays, for example, a February program may involve looking for portraits of presidents. To celebrate the photography of Ansel Adams, the day may include stories of the Wild West, lasso roping demonstrations and Native American dancing. During "DIY" or Do-it-Yourself weekends, you can follow a list of suggested activities in a guide and follow up with hands-on activities in the Education Workshop.

If you can't make one of these events, you can still create a fun family adventure by sharing your enthusiasm for art with your children. The permanent collection at the Corcoran, one of the few large, private museums in Washington outside the Smithsonian family,

MAKE THE MOST OF YOUR TIME

Corcoran's Sunday Traditions are a tradition for many local families, so registration is required. You can—and many parents do—sign up five weeks in advance. In fact, it's best to call at least four weeks ahead if possible or the hot-ticket program you want may be full.

EATS FOR KIDS

The Corcoran Gallery's **Café des Artistes** looks too elegant for little children, but high chairs and a kids' menu let you know that even the littlest child is welcome. The Corcoran's Jazz Gospel Brunch on Sunday is festive for families. If you'd rather dine on paper plates than china, **Burrito Brothers** (1825 I St. NW, tel. 202/887–8266), a Mexican fast-food restaurant, is a few blocks away in the Ronald Reagan Building.

numbers more than 14,000 works, including paintings by the first great American portraitists: John Singleton Copley, Gilbert Stuart, and Rembrandt Peale. In fact, the portrait on the $1 bill was modeled on Stuart's *Portrait of George Washington*. A replica (by the artist's own hand, not a copy by someone else) is at the gallery. Photography and works by contemporary American artists are also strengths here. If your children appreciate beauty, see the 13th-century stained-glass window that originally hung in France's Soissons Cathedral. When the sun shines, watch the colors seemingly melt onto the floor. Cartoon fans should check out the collection by French caricaturist Honoré Daumier. The exaggerated facial features in his caricatures of politicians eventually got him in trouble. (A little worse than being grounded—he went to jail.) Show little detectives the buffalo hunt in *Last of the Buffalo,* by Albert Bierstadt. See if they can find a coyote, a prairie dog, an elk, and antelopes.

If you like this sight you may also like the National Museum of Women in the Arts (#26).

KEEP IN MIND I thought it would be cool to take my kids and their cousins to the Corcoran. It was, until we got to the Salon Doré where the guards were practically stalking us. Looking back, I can't blame them. After all, it may not have been too wise of me to take three children under the age of five into a gilded room even if the walls displayed sports equipment and musical instruments.

DAR MUSEUM

Move over Paul Revere or, better yet, dismount! Docents at the DAR (Daughters of the American Revolution) Museum love to share the legend of Sybil Ludington. At 16, Sybil was said to have taken off on her horse to warn folks that the British had come to Danbury, Connecticut. Legend has it that Sybil rode sidesaddle on a big bay horse for 40 mi—26 mi more than Revere—through a dangerous no-man's land between British and American lines. Whether her story is true or not, scholars don't know. The daring deeds of women were rarely documented during the days of the Revolutionary War, but a statue and painting of Sybil are in the museum.

Modern kids discover what life was like 150 years or so B.C. (before computers) as part of the Colonial Adventure program (two week advance reservation required). The journey begins with dressing the part. Boys wear vests and three-corner caps. Girls don long white aprons, because proper Colonial ladies never showed their ankles.

MAKE THE MOST OF YOUR TIME If your children have particular interests, inform your docent. Kids with an ear for music should see the antique instruments in the Rhode Island room. In wealthy homes, parents often encouraged their daughters to play a keyboard instrument and their sons to play the flute or violin.

Docents, who are all DAR members and who also wear Colonial garb, lead tours tailored to different age groups; your younger offspring are encouraged to tour the museum separately from you and your older kids.

Your kids might think the Oklahoma room, set up like a Colonial kitchen, is cool. (Try to find a toaster.) The Georgia room depicts a Savannah tavern, where citizens gathered for the state's first reading of the Declaration of Independence. In the New Hampshire room, docents describe 18th- and 19th-century dolls. And the Wisconsin room depicts a one-room house like those that only quite fortunate families could afford in Colonial times. Your children might just leave the DAR Museum not only with an understanding of Colonial life but also with an appreciation of contemporary life.

If you like this sight you may also like the Children's Museum of Rose Hill Manor Park (#62).

KEEP IN MIND
I found one of the best parts of Colonial Adventure was actually getting a tour of the museum without having to entertain my little ones, but, alas, the worst part was not getting to be with them when they were all dressed up for their tour.

EATS FOR KIDS Kids might not care that Clara Barton was known as the Angel of the Battlefield and founder of the American Red Cross, but they may appreciate getting a bite to eat at the café named for her located in the American Red Cross building (1730 E St. NW), open 7–2, Monday through Friday. The lines are short, but the list of selections is long at the **Bread Line** (1751 Pennsylvania Ave. NW, tel. 202/822–8900), where you can get smoothies, sandwiches, and fresh-baked breads, bagels, and muffins on weekdays.

D.C. DUCKS

57

What do you get when you cross a tour bus with a boat? A duck, of course—that is, a D.C. Duck. Your family can tour the city by both land and water without leaving your seats aboard these unusual amphibious vehicles: standard 2½-ton GM trucks in water-tight shells with propellers and seats for 28 intrepid passengers.

During the 1½-hour ride, a wise-quacking captain entertains with anecdotes and historical trivia about Washington's memorials, monuments, and historic buildings. The captain may even quiz kids about sights along the way. Answer correctly and ding—the bell rings! For example, the captain may ask what boats are represented by the three flags near the statue of Christopher Columbus in front of Union Station. No, the answer isn't the *Love Boat*, the S.S. *Minnow*, and the *Titanic*, but rather the *Nina*, the *Pinta*, and the *Santa María*. But the part of the tour that quacks kids up the most is quacking themselves—both at tourists in town and real ducks on the water.

KEEP IN MIND Midway through the ride, the captains pass out "quackers." These bright yellow blowers look like bright orange beaks and they sound like ducks. It's all good and fun until you try to take the "quackers" away when you're off the boat!

MAKE THE MOST OF YOUR TIME If your family is more into bikes than boats or if you'd just like to tour the city a different way, consider a Bike the Sites Tour (1100 Pennsylvania Ave., tel. 202/842–2453; www.bikethesites.com). For $40 per adult, $30 for kids 12 and under (including use of a bike), you can take a 3-hour tour covering approximately 8 mi and 55 sights. Along the way, a guide discusses history, lore, and even scandals of the capital city. The trip is appropriate for ages 7 and older, and reservations are recommended.

Union Station main entrance,
Massachusetts Ave. NE near
N. Capitol St. Metro: Union Station

 202/966-3825;
www.dcducks.com

$29 ages 13 and up,
$15 children 4–12

 Apr–Oct, daily 10–5 (occasionally later);
M–F departures hourly, Sa–Su every ½ hr
(tickets available beginning at 9 AM)

 4 and up

Ducks, known as DUKWs in World War II, were created to transport soldiers and supplies from ships to areas without ports. During the war more than 21,000 DUKWs were produced, mostly by women. After the war, the Army left many DUKWs abroad, and they can still be found around the world.

Starting along the city streets, the Duck keeps pace with traffic. Eventually it moves into the Potomac River, from which your children can glimpse the Pentagon, the Anacostia Helicopter Station (home of the presidential helicopters), and the War College, formerly Fort McNair, where the conspirators who plotted to kill Lincoln were tried, convicted, and hanged. Often children are invited to take the captain's seat and steer the Duck.

If you like this ride you may also like the carousel at Glen Echo Park (#51).

EATS FOR KIDS Duck into Union Station, a bustling train station where inaugural balls have been held. More than 35 vendors offer fast food from around the world. If you prefer a restaurant, try **America** (tel. 202/ 682–9555), whose menu of regional foods lives up to the expansive name. Kid-pleasing offerings include peanut butter with marshmallow cream sandwiches. In November and December, request gallery seating for a bird's-eye view of the station's Holiday train exhibit.

DISCOVERY CREEK CHILDREN'S MUSEUM

Would your children like to play dirt detectives? Romp in a swamp? Build a volcano? Watch a chameleon change colors? Discovery Creek's innovative nature programs combine outdoor adventures, art projects or experiments, and live animal demonstrations. Weekdays are primarily devoted to school groups during the school year and a camp in summer, but on weekends the museum hosts drop-in (not drop-off) programs for families.

Discovery Creek, in historic Glen Echo Park (*see* #51), was once home to horses. The paddock has been transformed into a children's botanical garden where kids can play in a heron's nest tree fort, a wetlands area with ponds, bamboo trails, an underground tunnel where they can see root systems of plants, and a climbing wall.

Although the horses are long gone, the museum still brings the outdoors—and its creatures—in. Museum programs reflect themes that change once a year. When the theme was "pollinators," large flowers were painted on the floor to the ceiling and bees buzzed

MAKE THE MOST OF YOUR TIME Combine your trip here with a puppet show, a play, a carousel ride, or playing on the monkey bars at Glen Echo. Only the most ambitious families can do everything! To ensure that your family has a good time, make sure everyone dresses for adventure; good walking shoes are essential. If your children are young, you may need to provide a hand when climbing down the steep trail and over the creek's stepping stones.

in and out of their own glass-enclosed hive connected to the outside. One of the smallest museums in the area, Discovery Creek provides an intimate place to learn. The scope of exploration isn't restricted, however, as every program takes advantage of a nature trail in the woods behind the museum. Hundreds of insects scurry around a fallen tree trunk, teaching about soil decomposition and animal habitats. A steep trail leads to Minnehaha Creek, where kids traverse stepping stones, searching for crayfish and other water-lovers.

The museum cares for a menagerie of animals, some of which were rescued and raised by friends of the museum. Along with the wildlife and plants in the forest, these critters provide exciting, tangible activities that help kids learn about nature.

If you like this sight you may also like Roosevelt Island (#18).

KEEP IN MIND Be prepared for the unexpected. A child (or parent) who is fascinated one minute could be frightened the next as a bird expands its wings or a snake uncurls.

EATS FOR KIDS Glen Echo Pizza & Subs (7307 MacArthur Blvd., tel. 301/263–0414), sells slices of pizza or thick french fries covered with ketchup, cheese, or barbecue sauce served in sturdy paper cups. About 2 mi from Glen Echo, kids like the organic lollipops at **Bethesda Co-op** (6500 Seven Locks Rd., Cabin John, tel. 301/320–2530), where the flavors range from traditional to the unexpected like buttered popcorn and PB&J.

DISCOVERY THEATER

In the midst of the mammoth museums on the Mall is a small theater that brings both our national heritage and other cultures to life. Here kids can delight in entertaining and educational performances, such as the antics of Robert Strong as he juggles bowling balls, bananas, and rakes. He even teaches a few tricks of the trade. On a more serious note, history opens up as kids watch plays such as *How Old is a Hero* about Ruby Bridges, and other children of the Civil Rights movement.

In the S. Dillon Ripley Center west of the Castle (*see* #63), Discovery Theater is the scene of plays, puppet shows, and storytelling. Puppeteers can be seen manipulating their puppets in the background. Young audiences are often encouraged to take part, too, by singing, clapping, or helping to develop characters and plots. And since you're never more than 10 rows away from the action at Discovery Theater, which seats up to 200 people, close encounters between the audience and actors are easy.

KEEP IN MIND Ride a painted pony—with stripes, polka dots, even clown faces on their saddles—on a carousel in front of the building. The lone dragon is the most desired mount and sometimes kids will let others ahead of them so they're first in line for the dragon on the next cycle.

MAKE THE MOST OF YOUR TIME The "Weekend" section of the *Washington Post* lists Discovery Theater performances as well as other kid-oriented shows around town. Whichever show you select, reservations are recommended as shows often sell out and walk up tickets are not guaranteed. Plan to arrive 15 minutes early. If you're attending a 10 AM show, go around to the west entrance in the Enid A. Haupt garden, where the doors open early for Discovery Theater patrons only. Otherwise, the building itself doesn't open until 10.

S. Dillon Ripley Center,
1100 Jefferson Dr. SW.
Metro: Smithsonian

202/633-8700;
www.discoverytheater.org

$5 ages 3 and up;
$6 18 and up

Late Sept–late July,
M–F 10 and 11:30, Sa 12

2½–14

Though most performances are geared to preschoolers through sixth graders, some are for older children and teens. Many of these performances are held in the 550-seat Baird Auditorium at the Museum of Natural History. Performances for older kids tend to be factually based presentations about historical figures or events. Past examples have included *Sister Rain, Brother Sun,* a puppet show; *Angel in the Battlefield,* a play about Clara Barton; and *Come Sign with Me,* by Fred Beam, a performer who is deaf.

Throughout the year, Discovery Theater celebrates cultural heritage. For example, in late September and October, Hispanic Heritage takes center stage, and in November, tales from Native Americans are highlighted. The most popular month for performances is February, when Black History Month is celebrated with songs, stories, and plays about cowboys, heroes, and more.

If you like this sight you may also like the plays and puppet shows at Glen Echo Park (#51).

EATS FOR KIDS For a hot pretzel or an ice cream, check out the street vendors in front of the building. For a complete meal, walk over to the National Air and Space Museum's restaurants about 5 minutes away. Across the Mall, both the National Museum of Natural History (#27) and the National Museum of American History (#30) have restaurants (*see* listings for each).

FORD'S THEATRE
NATIONAL HISTORIC SITE

The events of April 14, 1865, which shocked the nation and closed this theater, continue to fascinate both young and old. On that night, during a performance of *Our American Cousin*, John Wilkes Booth entered the state box on the balcony and assassinated Abraham Lincoln. The stricken president was carried across the street to the house of tailor William Peterson, where he died the next morning.

Allow about half an hour to take a self-guided tour of Ford's Theatre and the Lincoln Museum (in the lower level) and to cross the street to Peterson House to see the bedroom where Lincoln died. (Allow more time during busy spring and summer months, since you may have to wait in line for a tour.) A Junior Ranger handout, aimed at kids 6–12, sends young history detectives on a hunt to find the box where Lincoln was shot, the Derringer pistol that Booth used, and the suit that Lincoln wore that night. The book also includes activities ranging from a connect-the-dots picture of Lincoln's top hat to word scrambles. After completing the activities, each child receives a Junior Ranger badge.

MAKE THE MOST OF YOUR TIME
Every year from Thanksgiving through New Year's, the ghosts of Christmases past, present, and future come to the Ford's Theatre stage in Charles Dickens's classic tale *A Christmas Carol*. (The rest of the year, performances tend to be serious adult plays.) Call 202/347–4833 for information.

Ford's Theatre: 511 10th St. NW;
Peterson House: 516 10th St. NW.
Metro: Metro Center

 Free

 Closed for renovation until late 2008. Daily 9–5; tours 15 min after the hr 9:15–4:15; theater closed during rehearsals and matinees (usually Th, Sa, and Su); call ahead.

202/426–6924;
www.nps.gov/foth

 7 and up

Throughout the day when the theater is open, National Park Service rangers and volunteers give 15-minute talks (some quite theatrical) about Lincoln's assassination. If you miss a presentation and your children have questions, encourage them to read the signs that accompany the displays in the museum (open even when the theater is not). Large type makes them more readable than typical museum signage. If you still have questions, talk to a ranger.

As of this writing, Ford's Theatre was slated to close in summer 2007 for an 18-month renovation. During this time, the Peterson House will remain open.

If your family likes this sight, they may also have interest in seeing the actual bullet that killed Lincoln, on display at the National Museum of Health and Medicine (#28).

KEEP IN MIND

How tall is your child? Probably not as tall as Abraham Lincoln, who was 6′4″—even more extraordinary in his day, because poor diet often stunted children's growth. Have your kid stand next to his full-size picture. Then take a photo of your child and Honest Abe.

EATS FOR KIDS Older kids love the **Hard Rock Cafe** (999 E St. NW, tel. 202/737–7625), which mixes rock memorabilia and tunes. For live tunes at lunchtime and lots of hot sandwiches, check out **Potbelly** (555 12th St., tel. 202/347–7100). The "Wreck®" is loaded with a variety of meat. The "Big Jack™" may sound intimidating but it's actually a classic PB&J. For kids who haven't graduated from the Wiggles to rock and roll or if there's a long wait, the food court at the **Old Post Office Pavilion** (1100 Pennsylvania Ave. NW, tel. 202/289–4224) may be better.

FRANKLIN DELANO ROOSEVELT MEMORIAL

If you visit this memorial to our 32nd president with older children, take your time walking through its four outdoor "rooms" or galleries—each symbolic of one of Roosevelt's four terms. Waterfalls and reflecting pools are interspersed throughout, which are good for dangling toes. Pause in the granite passageways between the galleries, engraved with some of Roosevelt's most famous quotes, including THE ONLY THING WE HAVE TO FEAR IS FEAR ITSELF. If you come with toddlers, however, head straight to the third room. Here, though youngsters can't sit on Roosevelt's lap, they can pet Fala, Roosevelt's Scottish terrier. The tips of Fala's ears shine from all the attention.

Assuming you come here for more than Fala, there's plenty to absorb. Challenge your children to look closely at the big bronze wall of faces in the second room; it depicts people put back to work after the Depression. See if you can find two men planting trees, an artist stirring paint, one farmer gathering oranges, and another driving a tractor. There's even a girl painting and a boy sculpting. Also in the second gallery, handprints along the columns, representing

MAKE THE MOST OF YOUR TIME This memorial presents one of the best places for family photographs. Have your child pet Fala, take a place in the Breadline, and listen to Roosevelt's fireside chat.

EATS FOR KIDS For refreshments, see the listing for the Lincoln Memorial (#44). A short drive away, **Maine Avenue Seafood Market** (1100 Maine Ave. SW) carries fresh fish and shellfish. Maine Avenue also contains seven waterside restaurants, including local seafood powerhouse **Phillips Flagship** (900 Water St. SW, tel. 202/488–8515). All have terraces overlooking the Washington Channel and the boats moored there.

1850 W. Basin Dr. SW, west side of Tidal Basin. Metro: Smithsonian

202/426–6841; www.nps.gov/fdrm

 Free

 24 hrs; staffed daily 9:30 AM–8 PM

 2 and up

the working hands of the American people, encourage you to touch. With help from parents, even babies can put their hands on prints. In the fourth room, a statue honors first lady Eleanor Roosevelt, a shy child who became a vocal spokesperson for human rights.

More than recognizing FDR's contributions, the memorial teaches children about history, war, and even disability. Due to polio, Roosevelt used a wheelchair for the last 24 years of his life, and a statue of him in a wheelchair was added to the memorial in 2001 after years of controversy. Ask an older child what's more important: that Roosevelt be seen realistically and as a role model for the disabled or that his desire not to have people see his disability be honored.

If you like this sight you may also want to see the original monument to Roosevelt in front of the National Archives Building (#36): It was made to order. Roosevelt said if anyone put up a memorial in his honor, he'd want it to be about the size of a desk.

KEEP IN MIND If the dog makes more of an impression on your little one than the president, many kids in the 1940s might have felt the same way. Fala was famous in his day. He sat at the feet of his master and British Prime Minister Winston Churchill when they signed the Atlantic Charter in 1941. For merchandise featuring the presidential pooch, check out the bookstore. A portion of the proceeds benefits the National Park Service.

FREDERICK DOUGLASS
NATIONAL HISTORIC SITE

Pick up tickets for the 30-minute tours in the visitor center, where a wall is devoted to this prolific speaker and writer's quotations. Among the more famous ones is, I WOULD UNITE WITH ANYBODY TO DO RIGHT AND WITH NOBODY TO DO WRONG. Here your children can shake hands with the bronze statue of Douglass, shiny gold from all the attention. The visitor center also has the Douglass family tree and a gift shop with books about Douglass.

Next you can watch the 17-minute film *Fighter for Freedom: The Frederick Douglass Story*. Douglass knew neither his mother, a slave, nor the identity of his father, a white man. At age 8, he was sent to work for a family in Baltimore, where he was exposed to the "mystery of reading" and decided that education was "the pathway to freedom." At 20 he escaped and became an abolitionist, women's rights activist, author, editor of an antislavery newspaper, minister to Haiti, and the most respected 19th-century African-American orator. After the film, follow a park ranger to Cedar Hill, the first designated African American National Historic Site and the last home of Frederick Douglass.

MAKE THE MOST OF YOUR TIME
Though *Fighter for Freedom: The Frederick Douglass Story* is enlightening, this short film depicts a graphic beating he got when he was a slave. Some children and even adults find it disturbing, not just because of the violence but because it confronts a shameful part of our history. Encourage your kids to talk about their feelings and ask questions of you and the rangers. To enhance your children's appreciation of Cedar Hill, talk about Frederick Douglass, the Civil War, and the Civil Rights movement before you arrive.

1411 W St. SE. Metro: Anacostia, then B2 bus

202/426-5961 or 202/619-7222; www.nps.gov/frdo

 Free, $1.50 per person for reservations. (Groups of less than 10, call 877/444-6777; more than 10 call 877/559-6777.)

 Mid-Apr–mid-Oct, daily 9–5 tours at 9, 12:15, 1:45, 3, 3:30, and 4); mid-Oct–mid-Apr, daily 9–4 (same tour start times, but the last tour begins at 3:30)

 9 and up

Your tour begins in front of the historic home, known as Cedar Hill, where Douglass lived from 1877 until his death in 1895. You'll not only see fancy four-poster beds, oil paintings, mahogany furniture, and beautiful china, but you will learn more about this remarkable man. Rangers focus on Douglass's life at Cedar Hill, first with Anna Murray, his wife of 40 years, and after her death, with second wife, Helen Pitts, who was not only 20 years his junior but also white. Douglass simply explained that his first wife was the color of his mother, his second the color of his father. Though the tour is best for children who have studied American history, rangers are skilled at engaging kids as young as kindergartners.

If you like this sight you may also like the Martin Luther King Jr. memorial on the Mall, slated for completion in 2008.

KEEP IN MIND
When my sons and I climbed the more than 80 stairs from the visitor center to Douglass's house, I thought about how I wanted them to appreciate Douglass's life. I think they did, but I must admit that they were just as fascinated to learn that Douglass slept sitting up.

EATS FOR KIDS Unfortunately, the only place you're allowed to eat here is on the grassy hill near the visitor center, next to the parking lot, but there are no picnic tables. So you might want to eat before or after your visit.

GLEN ECHO PARK

Years ago, Washingtonians took the trolley to Glen Echo's amusement park. Though neither the amusement park nor the trolley survived (and the closest Metro isn't close), Glen Echo, on the D.C. border, is still a magnificent and easily accessible park. It offers kids almost as many choices of activities as the historic Dentzel Carousel, in the park's center, offers choices of mounts, which range from a painted pony and a majestic lion to a saber-toothed tiger and an ostrich.

The arts thrive here. The Adventure Theater stages such children's productions as *Go Dog Go*, *The Stinky Cheese Man*, and *Winnie the Pooh* weekends year-round in a 170-seat theater that opened in 2007. At the Puppet Co. Playhouse, skilled puppeteers manipulate a variety of puppets in classic plays and stories in a theater that was made specifically for puppet shows. Twice a month, the Playhouse hosts Tiny Tot Tuesdays for wee ones up to 4 years old ($5 for all ages). *Nutcracker*, in winter, is one of the most popular productions.

MAKE THE MOST OF YOUR TIME Whatever event you're going to at Glen Echo, allow at least an extra 30 minutes. Just stomping over the bridge leading to the park takes time. You also may want to act out the Norwegian folktale of Billy Goats Gruff, toss stones in the creek, and take a spin around the carousel.

EATS FOR KIDS When the carousel at Glen Echo is open (May–Sept, W–Th 10–3 and Sa–Su 12–6, Sept–Oct, Sa–Su 12–6), so is the adjacent **snack bar.** But whether you bring or purchase food, you'll find enough picnic tables and wide-open spaces here to accommodate scores of families.

7300 MacArthur Blvd.,
at Goldsboro Rd., Glen Echo, MD

 301/634-2222 (24-hr info);
301/634-2229 (visitor information);
www.glenechopark.org

Clara Barton
National Historic
Site free; carousel
$1; puppet shows
$8 or plays $10

Daily 9–5; puppet shows W–F 10 and 11:30,
Sa–Su 11:30 and 1; plays Sa–Su 11 and 1:30

 All ages, plays 4–12

Sometimes puppeteers greet children after the shows. Reservations are recommended for this popular puppet place that seats 250.

Nature holds its own at Glen Echo Park. In the former stables, a Discovery Creek Children's Museum (see #56) offers nature programs, crafts, and outdoor adventures. History has its place, too, and children who have studied the Civil War or women's history may enjoy a tour of the Clara Barton National Historic Site, near the park entrance. Known as the "angel of the battlefield" for nursing wounded soldiers, Clara Barton founded the American Red Cross. Rangers conduct hourly tours that give insight into her life and Glen Echo at the turn of the last century. A stop into the Clara Barton House will give your kids a taste of how people recycled a century ago: Newspapers weren't put out in bins to be collected in front of your house; they were put into the house as insulation.

If you like this sight you might also like the plays at Discovery Theater (#55).

KEEP IN MIND The park is also a great spot for recreation. When your kids need to let off steam, there's plenty of space to run around and a playground with swings and slides. Also, there's more than kids' activities at this park, founded by two brothers who invented the egg beater. It's the adults who kick up their heels in the historic Spanish Ballroom. All dance events are open to the public, and most include a mini-lesson.

GODDARD SPACE FLIGHT CENTER

Not nearly as glitzy, large, or crowded as the Smithsonian's National Air and Space Museum (#39), this NASA-run museum brings space flight down to earth while letting imaginations soar. Though the center wasn't designed specifically for children, toddlers will love fiddling with the many controls that accompany the exhibits and turning on spacesuits.

The replica of the *Gemini XII* where astronauts Buzz Aldrin and Jim Lovell spent four days is as good as real for youngsters because they can go inside this compact car-size capsule and play with 100 buttons and knobs (count them!). Kids who want to look authentic can even wear spacesuits from a dress-up area.

After a trip aboard the *Gemini,* older kids may want to go on a scavenger hunt to find the speed of light (Hint: Faster than a toddler grabs a cookie), the color of young stars (pick from a patriotic palate), and other trivia. Winners take home a free lithographic of rockets

MAKE THE MOST OF YOUR TIME
Would your child like to practice reciting a countdown to takeoff or learn the basics of rocketry? On the first Sunday of each month from 1 to 2, Goddard goes overboard with outdoor rocket launches. You can even bring your own rocket (available at Goddard's gift shop), but know that you'll need about a half hour to assemble the rocket and 24 hours to let the glue dry.

Bldg. 88, Explorer Rd., Greenbelt, MD

 Free

Sept–June, T–F 10–3, Sa–Su 12–4; July–Aug, T–F 10–5, Sa 12–4; group tours by reservation only; closed on all federal holidays

301/286–9041; www.nasa.gov/goddard

2 and up, tours 9 and up

and space shuttles, a patch commemorating the Hubble Space telescope, or some other small flight memento.

When Goddard has enough staff and enough people in the Center, they'll show you Science on a Sphere. Using computers and video projectors, you can see animated images of the globe, the sun, and the stars.

Outside the center is a "rocket garden," with a real 92-foot Delta rocket and other authentic space hardware. You can also see other buildings at this sprawling government complex where scientists and engineers monitor spaceships circling the Earth, the solar system, and beyond.

If you like this sight you may also like the College Park Aviation Museum (#60).

KEEP IN MIND

Goodard is about 9 mi from Washington, but off the beaten path. From the Baltimore–Washington Parkway (I–295) or Capital Beltway, exit to Route 193 east (Greenbelt Road). Pass the Goddard Space Flight Center, continue ¾ mi to Soil Conservation Road, and turn left. Take the next left on Explorer Road, and follow signs.

EATS FOR KIDS Check out the display of fast food for space flight. Then to taste the real thing, purchase astronaut's freeze-dried ice-cream sandwiches in foil pouches at the gift shop. It's messy and not particularly tasty but still cool to kids. Picnicking is permitted on the grounds, but the only food sold here is soda from a vending machine. A short drive away in historic Greenbelt, the **New Deal Café** (113 Center Way, tel. 301/474–5642) gives parents a break. While waiting for your soups, sandwiches, or vegetarian—even vegan—entrées, your kids can read books, play board games, or work on puzzles.

GREAT FALLS

Thanks to the Ice Age two million years ago, a wide, flat, slow-moving body of water cut its way through bedrock and created Great Falls, a lovely waterfall on the Potomac adjacent to the C&O Canal National Historical Park. Here the water thrashes about faster, frothier, and noisier than the wildest bubble bath, although your kids might want to test that theory come bath time!

For information and a trail map, head to the 1831 tavern, which still welcomes visitors, though it stopped providing food and shelter in the 1930s. Scheduled to reopen in 2008 after renovation, the exhibits will cover how a lock works, plant and animal life, and more, but the main attraction at this park is the great outdoors.

KEEP IN MIND

The same mules that take visitors on a boat ride through the lock at the Chesapeake & Ohio (C&O) Canal (#64) work here, too. Rides are $7 ages 15 and up and $5 for children 4–14. The mules usually work April through October but call ahead for dates and times.

If it's hiking you're after, check out these interesting options, but beware of trails too rugged for little ones. The Billy Goat Trail sounds simple, but the 4-mi loop requires scrambling over boulders. Hiking boots and athletic ability are recommended. The Gold

MAKE THE MOST OF YOUR TIME

You can enjoy the falls from either Maryland or Virginia (9200 Old Dominion Dr., McLean, VA, tel. 703/285–2964). The Virginia side offers more opportunities for serious rock climbers. Bring your own equipment and register at the visitor center. Swimming and wading are prohibited on both sides, but you can fish (license required for anglers 16 and older), climb rocks, or go white-water kayaking—experienced boaters and below the falls only, as currents are deadly. Despite signs and warnings, people occasionally dare the water, and lose.

11710 MacArthur Blvd., Potomac, MD

 301/299-3613
or 301/767-3714;
www.nps.gov/choh

$5 vehicles, $3 per person
without vehicle, good for
3 days for visiting both
sides of the Falls, in MD
and VA

Park daily sunrise–sunset;
tavern daily 9–4:45

 4 and up

Mine Loop also runs about 4 mi, revealing the remains of an 1867–1939 mine. Not everyone went to California for gold. Sorry, panning isn't allowed today.

For a golden view of the falls that everyone enjoys, take the walkway to Olmsted Island. This 0.6-mi, wheelchair- and stroller-accessible route leads to a platform with a spectacular view of the churning waters. Along the walkway, signs alert you to ancient plants growing among the rocks. You might also see more recent arrivals: freshwater Asiatic clamshells, first reported here in the 1980s. In any case, your kids can find a cozy seat on the rocks in the middle of the platform or on the benches, and you can see Mother Nature at her wildest and woolliest.

If you like this sight you may also like the C&O Canal (#64) in Georgetown.

EATS FOR KIDS As at all National Park Service sights, you may not feed the animals, but you can feed yourselves. Buy something at the **snack bar** (open Mar–Nov), a few paces north of the tavern, or bring your own picnic. Potomac Village, 3½ mi away, has two supermarkets that sell prepared foods: **Giant** (9812 Falls Rd., tel. 301/983–4246) and **Safeway** (10104 River Rd., tel. 301/983–2150). Or take off for **Flaps** (10134 River Rd., tel. 301/983–2660), where miniature airplanes float overhead and kids can order anything from pasta with butter to lobster salad.

HIRSHHORN MUSEUM
AND SCULPTURE GARDEN

Any child who thinks art museums only display boring, two-dimensional paintings of old-fashioned people is in for a surprise at the Hirshhorn. Art here isn't only paint on canvas. Some art is made from mud, twigs, leaves, stone, light, video monitors, and even fat. Here a brightly colored fish mobile made of metal and glass swims. A wet dog in bronze walks. Paper flowers grow out of a wall.

American artists such as Georgia O'Keeffe, Jackson Pollock, Mark Rothko, and Frank Stella are represented along with modern European and Latin masters, including Juan Muñoz, René Magritte, and Joan Miró. Contemporary pieces by Robert Gober, Ann Hamilton, Jim Hodges, Ed Ruscha, Andy Warhol, and numerous others reflect the diversity of technique and expression of today's artists. Through acquisitions, the Hirshhorn continually adds work to the collection. Contemporary pieces by John Baldessari, Ann Hamilton, Jim Hodges, Ernesto Neto, and Lorna Simpson reflect a diversity of techniques.

MAKE THE MOST OF YOUR TIME Some of the coolest art for kids is outside in the Sculpture Garden. *Man Passing Through the Door* by Jean Ipousteguy may remind "muggles" of when Harry Potter boarded the train to Hogwarts, though instead of an owl, said man has another animal with him. Also: Ask your kids to find Kenneth Snelson's tall sculpture *Needle Tower* in the plaza. Get in its center, and look up. You'll see a star.

Independence Ave. at 7th St. SW.
Metro: Smithsonian or L'Enfant Plaza,
Maryland Ave. exit

 202/633-3382 or 202/633-1000,
202/357-1729 TTY; www.Hirshhorn.si.edu

 Free

Daily 10-5:30; Sculpture Garden
daily 7:30-sunset

 5 and up; Young at Art
3-12; Artlab 13-18

Visit the information desk for a free "Family Guide." It's full of colorful art cards that encourage your children to search for a work and relate it to their own lives and imagination. For example, on the card about Claes Oldenburg's *Geometric Mouse: Variation 1, Scale A,* kids are challenged to wonder what it would be like to be a geometric mouse visiting a mouse house with 500 other geometric mice. To design a tour for your family, allow your kids to choose their own art cards and go to the youngest child's selections first.

The Hirshhorn's ArtLab (just off the Sculpture Garden) offers classes taught by professional artists and art educators. Throughout the year children and their parents can drop in for a few minutes or hours for Gallery Tales for Tots and hands-on art projects inspired by work on view in the galleries.

If you like this sight you may also like the National Gallery of Art (#33).

KEEP IN MIND The Hirshhorn suggests that you connect artworks with experiences meaningful to your child. Pablo Picasso's *Woman with a Baby Carriage,* also on the third floor, might elicit a story about pushing your own baby in a carriage. Although children are encouraged to get to know the art, please remind your kids not to get too friendly. The artwork is for the eyes, not the fingers.

EATS FOR KIDS
When the Hirshhorn opened in 1974, detractors who didn't like the cylindrical architecture of the museum called it the Doughnut on the Mall. If you're looking for a doughnut or other goodie to eat, check out ideas under the (Smithsonian) Castle (#63).

INTERNATIONAL SPY MUSEUM

Whether they're eavesdropping on siblings or searching for hidden presents, kids love to spy. This museum takes the art of espionage to new levels for junior James Bonds and young Nancy Drews.

Did you know there are more spies in Washington than in any other city? Crowds of curious visitors walk through metal detectors and watch a short video on espionage before winding through the exhibits. Like little moles, kids can crawl through the museum's ductwork to peek through the vents. They find larger-than-life-size silver flies on walls that transmit information to undisclosed locations.

Despite all the cool gadgetry that makes kids want to speed too quickly in hot pursuit of adventure through the museum, take your time when you see the replica of James Bond's Aston Martin sports car. Just like in the films, gadgets galore pop out.

EATS FOR KIDS It's no secret that the museum's **Spy City Cafe** (tel. 202/654–0995) serves killer sandwiches, wraps, salads, and a large selection of cookies from molasses ginger to white-chocolate macadamia nut. To pursue predictable fare, cross the street to **Subway** (901 E St., tel. 202/737–3480).

MAKE THE MOST OF YOUR TIME At peak times—spring and summer weekends, Thanksgiving, and Christmas—the museum recommends buying tickets through their Web site at least 48 hours in advance. The high-tech feel of this metallic and wood museum is particularly cool for preteens and teenagers. If you bring along a younger sibling, your child might not be only one who gets tired, as seating is limited and strollers aren't allowed in the museum (nor are food, beverages, or cameras).

800 F St. NW. Metro:
Gallery Place/Chinatown

 $18 adults,
$15 children age 5–11,
free for children
under 5

 Jan–mid-March, Sept–Dec, daily 10–6; mid-March–
mid-April, daily 9–8; mid-April–mid-Aug, daily 9–7;
mid-late Aug daily 10–7; periodic special hours
Saturdays

202/393–7798;
www.spymuseum.org

 10 and up

Watch as people transform themselves into spies on videos that made Superman's telephone booth transition look way too simple. Through wardrobe changes, makeup, facial hair, and shoe inserts to make a person limp, a man and a woman transformed themselves into people their own close friends probably couldn't recognize.

While the museum offers clues and commentary on the capture of John Hanssen, Aldrich Ames, and other modern spies, a professional spy from the 12th century may draw just as much interest. In a huge glass cage, a life-size figure of a masked Ninja poses, representing the Japanese art of invisibility. Other tricks of the trade include homing pigeons with cameras, a pistol in a lipstick, and a spy kit with ropes, candles, flashlights, pliers, rubber gloves, and more.

If you like this sight you may also like the National Air and Space Museum (#39).

KEEP IN MIND For teens who want to put their sleuthing skills to work, they can crack a safe, conduct a polygraph of a suspect, weigh evidence and more through Operation Spy. This one-hour program debuted in 2007 to give participants (12 and older) a chance to "feel, think, and act" like real intelligence officers. Operation Spy costs an additional $14 per person (combination tickets with admission available) and reservations are not required, but recommended. The spies work in groups of about 15. Operations run about every 10 to 15 minutes.

KENILWORTH NATIONAL
AQUATIC GARDENS

hildren like to run through this 12-acre national park devoted to aquatic plants. However, the best way to enjoy this sanctuary is to walk quietly and pause often. Hear bullfrogs croak and birds chirp, search for turtles and frogs among platter-size leaves, gaze upon exotic plants and water lilies reminiscent of a Monet painting. A clever game of "I Spy" might slow the kids down enough for the park's true pleasure—bird-watching. With red-wing blackbirds, blue herons, and bald eagles there's plenty to spy.

Ask your youngsters how cattails and yellow flag irises got their names or whether pickerelweeds and rose mallow shrubs (no relation to marshmallows) look as silly as they sound. Watch for frogs jumping onto lily pads, turtles sunbathing, and crayfish burrowing mud chimneys to escape from turtles and birds. Don't restrict yourselves to sight and sound: Let your other senses, like touch and smell (tasting isn't recommended), help you explore the park, too.

KEEP IN MIND Driving directions are tricky; it's best to call ahead. If you do get lost, you should know that locals refer to Kenilworth as "lily ponds." Keep a careful eye on children, especially preschoolers, while they search for aquatic life. Although the ponds are only 3 feet deep, the banks can be slick and there are no fences around them. The only barriers are those in the ponds, designed to protect the plants. And don't worry if your clothes get a little dirty. It's all part of the fun.

1550 Anacostia Ave. NE

 202/426-6905;
www.nps.gov/kepa

 Free

Daily 7–4

2 and up

Pick up maps at a tiny visitor center: one for the ponds and one for the Anacostia River trail, at whose end you can see beaver hutches at low tide. Incidentally, unlike the beavers that gnawed down cherry trees on the Mall in 1999, the Kenilworth beavers are helpful. By dining on water lilies, they keep the plants from getting too crowded to flower.

For young children, ask for a treasure list, which changes every few months. In winter, you can search for the shells of pond crustaceans left by birds and follow animal tracks. Do you think the bird got away, or did the fox eat last night? In spring, you may hunt for muskrat holes in the dikes or watch female dragonflies dip their tails in the water to lay eggs. Whatever the season, it's fun watching kids explore Kenilworth.

If you like this sight you may also like the U.S. National Arboretum (#9).

MAKE THE MOST OF YOUR TIME

The best time to visit is 8–11, when day-bloomers are opening and night-bloomers have yet to close. Water lilies flower through the summer.

EATS FOR KIDS Beavers not only enjoy munching on the bark of trees, they like to munch on the roots of the water lilies, which is why the more exotic varieties are near the visitor center. Alas, there's no food for humans here and there aren't any restaurants within walking distance of these gardens tucked away in a corner of Northeast Washington. The only food or drink available here is a water fountain at the visitor center. Pack a big lunch and take advantage of the picnic tables near the ponds.

THE KENNEDY CENTER

The Kennedy Center looks like a place for adults in tuxedos and black dresses, and it is. But it's also a place that rolls out the red carpet for children. As the nation's performing-arts center, it takes seriously its responsibility to make an eclectic calendar of top-notch performances accessible to many. One example is the dark-red Show Shuttle, which runs between the center and the Foggy Bottom Metro every 15 minutes.

More than 100 family events are held each year through the Center's Performances for Young Audiences in which actors, dancers, storytellers, musicians, and puppeteers show off for kids. The National Symphony Orchestra puts on Kinderkonzerts and family concerts. Arrive 45 minutes early before most shows and your children can beat drums, blow into a tuba, or clang cymbals. Tots and their stuffed animal friends love the popular Teddy Bear Concerts where musicians play on tiny versions of their instruments—like the ones they used when they were little.

MAKE THE MOST OF YOUR TIME Cue sheets for many children's performances are available on the Kennedy Center's Web site. Not only do the sheets provide background information on the performers and their art, but they often give kids a list of things to look for when watching a show.

EATS FOR KIDS For restaurants with a view, you can't beat the top of the Kennedy Center. The **KC Café** offers self-serve soup, sandwiches, pasta salads, and pizza overlooking the Potomac and Georgetown. The formal **Roof Terrace Restaurant** isn't appropriate for most kids, but for older children with tickets to a play, it could be a great way to start the evening. Prices at both the café and the restaurant tend to be steep, but the service is quick, ensuring that you get to the show on time!

As part of the Performing Arts for Everyone Initiative, free one-hour performances are held nightly at 6 on the Millennium Stage (neither ticket nor reservation required). Many provide the perfect opportunity to introduce children to classical music or opera. In others, dancers, actors, storytellers, or magicians reach out to kids of all ages. Performers have included Frank Sinatra Jr. and the Duke Ellington Orchestra, as well as local artists. Seats are generally plentiful, though kids often sit up front or on the steps, or they don't sit at all—they dance!

Even without seeing a performance, however, you can enjoy this six-theater memorial to President Kennedy. Pick up a "flag sheet" at the information desk, and visit the Hall of Nations and Hall of States, where the flags of more than 140 countries and all 50 states hang, the latter in order of admission to the union.

If you like this sight you might also like the National Cathedral (3101 Wisconsin Ave. NW, 202/537–6200, www.cathedral.org), also immense and awe-inspiring.

KEEP IN MIND The 618-foot-long Grand Foyer carpeted in red is a tempting place for kids to run. It's easy to understand why. The Foyer is one of the world's largest rooms. If you could lay the Washington Monument on its side in the Grand Foyer, you would still have about 3 inches to spare. Look up, and you'll see tons of crystal—literally. Each of the 18 chandeliers weighs 1 ton.

LINCOLN MEMORIAL

Give your kids five, as in five dollars. Or give them a penny. Either way, they'll see a picture of the Lincoln Memorial. Then take them to the real thing.

Children eager to show off newly acquired counting skills will find plenty to keep them busy here. Thirty-six Doric columns, representing the 36 states in the country at the time of Lincoln's death, surround the somber statue of the seated Lincoln. Above the frieze are the names of the 48 states of the union when the memorial was dedicated in 1922. (Alaska and Hawaii are noted by an inscription on the terrace leading up to the memorial.)

Older children may practice their oratorical skills by reciting two of Lincoln's great speeches—the Second Inaugural Address and the Gettysburg Address—which are carved on the north and south walls. Kids can even find the exact spot (look down for the engraving added in 2003) on the steps of the Lincoln Memorial where Martin Luther King Jr. gave his famous "I Have a Dream" speech in 1963.

MAKE THE MOST OF YOUR TIME Though many visitors look only at the front and interior of the monument, there is much more to explore. On the lower level, to the left of the main stairs, is Lincoln's Legacy, a display that chronicles the memorial's construction. A video and photos depict famous demonstrations and speeches that have taken place here, and another exhibit shows postage stamps from around the world that feature Lincoln on them.

Look carefully at Lincoln's face and hands. They look especially lifelike because they were based on castings done of Lincoln while he was president. Those who know sign language might recognize that Lincoln's left hand is shaped like an A while his right hand looks like an L. Although it's a myth that this was done on purpose, Daniel Chester French, the sculptor, had a son who was deaf.

If you don't need to get home for an early bedtime, we strongly recommend you visit at night, one of the best times to see the memorial. The drama and awe are palpable as spotlights illuminate the exterior, whereas inside, light and shadows play gently across Lincoln's face.

If you like this sight you might also like Ford's Theatre National Historic Site (#54).

EATS FOR KIDS

A **refreshment stand** (French Dr., north side of Independence Ave. SW) serves sandwiches, fries, chicken fingers, just a short walk from the memorial.

KEEP IN MIND Consider bringing your kids back at night in their pajamas for a "Goodnight, Mr. Lincoln" tour, run by Washington Walks (202/484–1565; www.washingtonwalks.com; $10 adults, $5 kids 12 and under, 3 and under free), every Saturday at 7 PM (Memorial Day through Labor Day). Participants learn what kind of bed young Abe slept in, what his pajamas were like, and whether or not he brushed his teeth before bed. The tour includes a bedtime story on why Lincoln grew a beard. Tuck-in is still up to you.

MADAME TUSSAUD'S
WASHINGTON, DC

Leave your autograph book at home, but grab your camera and get up close and personal with the famous and infamous. Though Madame Tussaud has been entertaining Europeans with wax portraits for more than 200 years, this Washington, D.C., showplace in the historic Woodward and Lothrop building opened in 2007.

You can take photographs of your family with a virtual who's who of movies, music, sports, and, of course, politics. Fifty uncannily lifelike wax portraits are featured in four themed, interactive exhibits. In Behind the Scenes, kids can see how the wax figures are made and can compare their hands, feet and even eyes to lifelike replicas of famous folk.

In Sports, kids can find out how much bigger they need to grow to measure up to Babe Ruth and putt with golfer Tiger Woods. In Glamour, kids might not know Brad Pitt or Julia Roberts, but they might recognize the president in The Spirit of Washington, DC. In a replica of the Oval Office, your daughter cannot only sit behind the desk, she can prop

MAKE THE MOST OF YOUR TIME You can save 15% off the admission if you bring your American Automobile Association (AAA) card (even though you'll probably take the Metro), but you might put those dollars toward buying an "official portrait" of your child with the president.

EATS FOR KIDS About two thirds of the way through the exhibit, *Sega Fredo Café* serves sandwiches, salads, and gelato. Enchiladas and tacos aren't the only dishes for kids at **Austin Grill** (750 E St. NW, 202/393–3776); kids can order PB&J or carrots and celery sticks. **Clyde's of Gallery Place (**707 7th St. NW, tel. 202/349–3700) is part of the Clyde's restaurant group that's been serving D.C. diners for generations.

1025 F St. NW. Metro: Metro Center.

 202/942-7300;
www.madame-tussauds.com

 $25 + tax ages 13 and up,
$18 + tax ages 4–12;
under 4 free

 10–6

 7 and up

her feet up on it (if her legs are long enough!). The Spirit section covers more than modern-day politics as kids can greet many of the men immortalized in memorials and monuments: Abraham Lincoln, Franklin Roosevelt, and Martin Luther King Jr. will be honored in a new memorial in the next couple of years.

After seeing all these famous folks, your child might want to brag about it, and she can tell more than her friends: At the final stop in Madame Tussaud's D.C., kids can tell all to Katie Couric, while parents and friends watch on a nearby TV monitor.

If you like this sight you may also like the Newseum (#23), which also gives kids a chance to appear on camera.

KEEP IN MIND Your kids might wonder who Madame Tussaud was. The young Marie learned her skills from a doctor. During the French Revolution, she was captured but managed to keep her head, along with her collection of death masks of guillotined nobles. She fled to England, where these gruesome models became a touring exhibition. In addition to this branch and the London original there are Madame Tussaud outposts in New York, Amsterdam, Las Vegas, Shanghai, and Hong Kong.

MEDIEVAL TIMES DINNER & TOURNAMENT

Young ladies and lords have a regal time at this replica of a Castle from the Middle Ages cast in the most modern of settings—a shopping mall.

Dine on an authentic medieval four-course feast while valiant knights on horseback compete in games of skill and jousting during a live two-hour performance.

Like any gracious host and hostess, the king and princess greet each guest upon arrival. Everyone receives a crown in a color that determines which of six knights you'll cheer for and where you'll dine in the 1,020-seat arena organized by colors (yellow; blue; black and white; red and yellow; red; and green). Some children may actually follow the plot during the two-hour performance. The king seeks revenge for the prince's death, a princess looks for love, and a wizard named Cedric warns of betrayal. Strobe lights, smoke, overture-type music add to the drama. Horses dance to waltzlike music. For most kids, the storyline is secondary to the action.

MAKE THE MOST OF YOUR TIME Medieval Times encourages guests to arrive one hour early. This gives you time to get crowned and browse in the gift shop (full of temptations like wooden swords, and costumes for squires and princesses). The Torture Chamber is small and definitely not for young children. But the $2 cover charge may be worth the price of admission for some preteens and teenagers who may be so grossed out by the replicas of these ancient devices that losing time on electronic toys or being grounded for a day would seem like a relatively mild punishment.

7000 Arundel Mills Circle, Hanover, MD (Arundel Mills Mall)

 888/935-6878; www.medievaltimes.com

 $48.95; $35.95 (12 and under); 3 and under sitting on laps free (taxes and gratuities not included)

 W–Th 7, F 7:30, Sa–Su 5 and 7:30 (more shows may be available); gift shop open mall hrs

 4 and up

Everyone is encouraged to root their knights on to victory and the crowd becomes boisterous as the battle begins. Knights on and off horses compete with each other to become the champion. Although the swords aren't sharp, they create sparks when they clash, and the stunts are real. With swords, axes, spears, shields, and even hand-to-hand combat, knights duke it out with one another. Notice the accuracy as the knights throw lances to one another while riding on the horses. They train by tossing water balloons back and forth! Maybe you'd be surprised to learn that some of the knights were recruited for their athleticism and didn't know how to ride horses. They start as squires and train for 8 to 12 months before becoming knighted by the king.

If you like this sight, you might also like riding horses at Rock Creek Park (#19).

KEEP IN MIND
Medieval Times is worth the drive from Washington for many kids, but if your child is fearful of the dark, you might want to skip it since a lot of the action takes place in semi-darkness.

EATS FOR KIDS Although this experience may seem royal, don't expect your kids to act too fine and fancy as they eat. They can't. Just as in the middle ages, they don't dine with silverware here either. All four courses are finger food, except for the soup, which you drink out of the bowl. Everyone is served the same fare regardless of age or preference. So if your kid wouldn't like the creamy tomato bisque, garlic bread, chicken, spare ribs, and herb-basted potato, you might want to factor in a trip to the Mall's food court. Also, the beverage choices are limited to soda, tea, and water.

MOUNT VERNON

How much does your child know about our first president? Chances are, not as much as you did when you were a kid. The people at Mount Vernon want to change that. A visit to Mount Vernon now offers much more than a chance to see George Washington's elegant and stately mansion. In 2007, the Ford Orientation Center and the Donald W. Reynolds Museum and Education Center opened, so visitors get to know the Washington who was not just a soldier, but an entrepreneur, a stepfather, and, even, a kid. In the orientation center, you can't miss Mount Vernon in Miniature. With a step up on the platform, even preschoolers can watch with everyone else as drawers open, windows open, and fireplaces glow in this exact replica of the mansion. Ask your child to remember a few details so you can compare the miniature version to the real home.

KEEP IN MIND The film *We Fight to be Free* in the Ford Orientation Center offers a wonderful overview of the estate and George Washington, but if your child is under six or afraid of loud noises, you won't want to stay past the first 15 minutes.

During the 30-minute tour of the mansion, interpreters tell about Washington's home and answer questions, and give you a sense of the country's first president. Upstairs, the

EATS FOR KIDS To protect Mount Vernon from damage and litter, food and beverages are not permitted on the grounds, but water fountains are near the mansion and all rest rooms. Popcorn (which George Washington ate), pizza (which he didn't), and more are available in the **food court pavilion** with indoor and outdoor seating in the Reynolds building. For a taste of Colonial life, try Colonial Turkey Pye (made of turkey and mixed veggies topped with a homemade buttermilk biscuit) or peanut and chestnut soup at the on-site **Mount Vernon Inn** (tel. 703/780–0011). The inn also offers modern meals, such as chicken fingers and hamburgers for kids.

South end of George Washington
Memorial Pkwy., Mt. Vernon, VA

 $13 ages 12 and up,
$6 children 6–11

 Mar, Sept, and Oct, daily 9–5; Apr–Aug,
daily 8–5; Nov–Feb, daily 9–4

 703/780–2000;
www.mountvernon.org

 3 and up

beds may look small, but that's an optical illusion resulting from their being high off the ground. The shortest mattress is 6'3", a tad longer than the general himself. Perhaps more interesting to kids than the house are a dozen meticulously restored outbuildings, including a major greenhouse, a kitchen, stables, and slave quarters.

The new Education Center's 16 galleries roughly follow a chronological view of Washington's life. Kids especially enjoy the animated cartoon of Washington's early life, Washington's false teeth, life-size images of Washington, and the movie in the "First in War Gallery" where the action on the screen is enhanced by falling snow, rumble seats, and fog. Especially useful for the child who must touch everything is the Hands-on History room, near the Visionary Entrepreneur exhibit in the Education Center. Kids can play games and dress up.

If you like Mount Vernon you may also like the Washington Monument (#6).

MAKE THE MOST OF YOUR TIME There's so
much to do, see, and learn here. You could easily spend a day here and not get bored. Mount Vernon is the most-popular historic home in the country. Tourists pull up by the busload in spring and summer. To beat the crowds, you could arrive late in the afternoon, but remember that the grounds close at 5. No matter what time of year you visit Mount Vernon, pick up an Adventure Map.

MYSTICS BASKETBALL

Kids don't need a wizard's wand or sorcerer's stone to enjoy the magic of the Mystics, Washington's popular WNBA team. Adults don't need a wad of money either. At a fraction of what it costs to watch the Wizards (Washington's NBA team), you can catch a family-friendly Mystics game at the Verizon Center, the 20,000-seat arena at the crossroads of Metro's red, green, and yellow lines.

Women have come a long way since they first dribbled basketballs in 1892, a year after the game was invented and nearly three decades before they won the vote. People could have hardly imagined a women's professional basketball league back in the early 1890s, when women wore floor-length dresses, even on the court. They gained more freedom in 1896, when they began playing in bloomers, loose-fitting trousers gathered at the knee. Now, of course, they, like men, dress for comfort and ease of motion when they play, sweating through plenty of socks (around 960!) each season.

KEEP IN MIND If you ever come for a Capitals game, you might want to visit the Hockey 101 booth, where team representatives answer your questions. For example, how many sticks do the players use? Some players may go through a couple per game, while others use one for a whole season. How do players sharpen their skates? They don't. The equipment manager sharpens them. If your kids are too young to ask questions, they might enjoy a hug from Slapshot, the Capitals' mascot. With a wingspan of 6 feet, this eagle can tickle your kids with his feathers.

601 F St. NW. Metro: Gallery Place/Chinatown

202/661-5000, www.washingtonmystics.com; Verizon Center, 202/661-5050, 877/DC HOOP www.verizoncenter.com

 $10-$38, depending on seat location

 Memorial Day–Labor Day, many games weekends

 5 and up

Meet outside section 109/110 before a game and kids can high-five players as they enter onto the court. The crowds go wild as the royal-blue, gold, and white-clad Mystics prove with each shot that they've got game. During the game, a panda named Pax and 25 Mayhem dancers, ages 7–18, cheer on the players and spread high-fives through the crowd. (Just think: 600 kids try out for the Mayhem.) During the game, other kids give out bangers (long balloons that when clapped together create a thunderous sound) that add to the excitement. Need another reason to see the Mystics? Tickets are easier to come by than for the NBA Wizards or the NHL Capitals.

If you like the Mystics, you might also like another testament to the power of women at the National Museum of Women in the Arts (#26).

MAKE THE MOST OF YOUR TIME

Gather a group of 20 or more and you not only qualify for discount tickets, you can have your group's message, such as "Happy Birthday" or "Congratulations," highlighted on the telescreen. A day's notice (tel. 202/661-5050) is all you need!

EATS FOR KIDS Eat at the game or stroll under the gold and red arch to Chinatown. The noodle chef entertains folks as he stretches dough into strips of pasta from the front window of **Chinatown Express** (746 6th St. NW, tel. 202/638-0424). Order your noodles with beef, chicken, or seafood. Or slurp them in a soup. **Tony Cheng's** (619 H St. NW, tel. 202/371-8669) offers barbecue on the first floor and traditional fare upstairs.

NATIONAL AIR AND SPACE MUSEUM

There's a good reason why this place is the most popular museum in the world: Kids love it. The 23 galleries here tell the story of aviation and space from the earliest human attempts at flight. Suspended from the ceiling like plastic models in a child's room are dozens of aircraft, including the actual Wright 1903 Flyer that Orville Wright piloted over the sands of Kitty Hawk, Charles Lindbergh's *Spirit of St. Louis*, the X-1 rocket plane in which Chuck Yeager broke the sound barrier, and the X-15, the fastest aircraft ever built.

Kids like walking through the backup model of the *Skylab* orbital workshop to see how astronauts live. At the How Things Fly gallery, children sit in a real Cessna 150 cockpit, "perform" experiments in midair. An activity board at the gallery entrance lists times for paper airplane contests and demonstrations by museum "Explainers," high school and college students who encourage kids to participate. At the Explore the Universe exhibit, kids learn how past stargazers mapped the heavens and what mysteries about our universe still remain. Don't let long lines deter you from seeing a show in the five-story Lockheed

KEEP IN MIND Consider dressing your children in identical colors so that you can spot them easily. Also, review safety rules ahead of time, and point out what the security officers are wearing (white shirts, navy slacks, and hats) so your children know whom to turn to if they get lost.

MAKE THE MOST OF YOUR TIME You're one in a million . . . make that six to nine million (depending on the year)—annual visitors, that is. The world's most popular museum is also thought to be Earth's most visited building. The museum is huge (three blocks) and popular. To avoid crowds, go early on a weekday morning or plan your visit for fall or winter. The tickets to film and planetarium shows sell out quickly so buy your tickets upon arrival (or in advance through the Web site).

Independence Ave. and 6th St. SW.
Metro: L'Enfant Plaza

202/633–1000, 202/633–5285–1729 TTY; theater,
planetarium 877/932–4634 or 202/633–4629;
www.nasm.si.edu

 Free

Daily 10–5:30

3 and up

Martin IMAX Theater. Films like *To Fly!* (a kids' favorite) make you feel you've left the ground. Strollers aren't allowed at the movies, but then kids under 4 may find the noise and larger-than-life images frightening anyway.

For a look at the final frontier, check out the Albert Einstein Planetarium. *Infinity Express,* a 20-minute tour of the universe and *Cosmic Collisions,* a film about the dynamic evolution of the universe are shown throughout the day. *The Stars Tonight,* for stargazers 6 and up, discusses at noon what you can expect to see in the current sky (Tuesday, Thursday, and Saturday). Before you leave, go to Milestones of Flight to touch the moon rock, one of only three on Earth you can feel.

If you like this sight you may also like the Steven F. Udvar-Hazy Center (#38).

EATS FOR KIDS Take your place in the **cafeteria** line for a bite of the most familiar restaurant food on earth—**McDonald's**—plus offerings from **Boston Market** and **Donatos Pizza**. Upstairs you can look out on the Mall, and the National Museum of the American Indian (#29). If you want a treat to take home, head to the tri-level gift shop, which sells such flight-related merchandise as freeze-dried astronaut food.

Like its older sibling (the Air and Space Museum on the Mall, #39), the Steven F. Udvar-Hazy Center tells the story of aviation and space exploration with displays of amazing aircraft and spacecraft. But this museum isn't divided into galleries. Instead, aircraft are displayed in huge open hangars on three levels under a ceiling that's 10 stories high.

This gargantuan Smithsonian facility displays more than 120 aircraft, 135 spacecrafts, rockets, satellites, and experimental flying machines, including a Concorde, the Space Shuttle Enterprise, the fabled Lockheed SR-71 Blackbird, which in 1990 flew from Los Angeles to Washington, D.C., in slightly over an hour, and the Enola Gay, which in 1944 dropped on Japan the first atomic devices to be used in war.

When you enter the building, you'll be in the Boeing Aviation Hangar, with civil aviation to the left and military aviation to the right. Straight ahead you'll see the Space Shuttle Enterprise.

MAKE THE MOST OF YOUR TIME
There's a $12 fee to park your car in the gigantic parking lot right in front of the museum. You really don't have any other parking options, so be prepared to pay the fee. The only way around it is to visit after 4 when parking is free. Other expenses might include an IMAX movie, a trip on a flight simulator, and a souvenir from the gift shop.

14390 Air and Space Museum Pkwy., Chantilly, VA

 Free (parking $12)

Daily 10–5:30; docent tours 10:30 and 1 (best for ages 10 and up)

202/633–1000; www.nasm.si.edu

 2 and up

The museum's wide aisles and cement floors are ideal for strollers and the planes are big enough that parents of toddlers don't have to hoist them up on their shoulders to see. (As a matter of fact, signs throughout the museum let you know that adults can't hold kids on their shoulders, for safety reasons.) Skywalks will take you nose-to-nose with the smaller aircraft suspended from the ceiling.

You can't miss the big stuff, but if you don't look carefully at the display cases you might skip some unexpected treasures, such as space toys, memorabilia from the days of Lindbergh-mania, personal items the astronauts carried, and a space-traveling spider named Anita.

If you like this sight you may also like the National Air and Space Museum (#39).

KEEP IN MIND
Check out the Discovery Carts throughout the center. You might just get to try on replicas of $20,000 space gloves while younger children can play with astronaut dolls. You also might learn how astronauts take care of elimination issues. (Think diapers.)

EATS FOR KIDS Like at a small airport, your choices are limited here. On-site, you can find a **McDonald's** and a **McCafé.** To take off for more options, go down Route 50 where you'll find local chain restaurants such as **Anita's** (13921 Lee Jackson Hwy., tel. 703/378–1717), with mini-tacos for kids, and national chains, such as **Bob Evans** (14050 Thunderbolt Pl., tel. 703/834–0511), where spaghetti is popular at lunch, but if you leave the site you can't reenter without paying for parking again so you may want to plan your visit so it doesn't conflict with lunch or snack time.

NATIONAL AQUARIUM

The basement of the Department of Commerce building is a strange address for a tourist attraction, but that's where you can find the nation's oldest public aquarium. Since the 1870s, it has housed interesting sea creatures, including a two-headed diamond terrapin in the 1940s, whose two heads would compete for the same morsel of food. Although you won't see any two-headed creatures or huge sharks that make a big splash, this museum's small size is a plus for parents of tots who want to find Nemo.

Unlike more modern aquariums, this one is small enough that you can circle through it in about 20 minutes. Aisles are wide enough for double strollers, and the aquarium isn't generally crowded. Nevertheless, more than 250 species and 1,700 specimens of aquatic life, including American alligators, spiny lobsters, venomous lionfish, clownfish, flesh-chomping piranhas, and their seaworthy mates swim here. Animals live in traditional rectangular tanks.

MAKE THE MOST OF YOUR TIME Also consider visiting Baltimore's glitzier National Aquarium (Pier 3, tel. 410/576–3800; www.aqua.org). An hour's drive from D.C. off-peak, it's Maryland's top tourist attraction. But be warned: It's more expensive and crowded than Washington's aquarium.

EATS FOR KIDS Sharks are fed at 2 on Monday, Wednesday, and Saturday. Piranhas are fed at 2 on Tuesday, Thursday, and Sunday. Alligators are fed at 2 on Friday. People can catch a bite to eat at any time at food courts in the lower level of the **Ronald Reagan Building** (1300 Pennsylvania Ave. NW, tel. 202/312–1300). On a pleasant day, consider walking over to the top level of the **Shops** (see the White House, #2).

14th St. and Constitution Ave. NW.
Metro: Federal Triangle

 202/482-2825;
www.nationalaquarium.com

 $5 ages 11 and up,
$2 ages 2–10

 Daily 9–5

 1 and up

The aquarium features habitats that represent the Office of National Marine Sanctuaries stretching from the Florida Keys to Fagatele Bay in American Samoa. Freshwater tanks focus on familiar friends such as turtles and newts, and a few unfamiliar fish, too. The boneytail chub, one of most rare fish in the Colorado River, is close to extinction because so many dams were built. This fish grows up to about 2 feet and may live more than 40 years.

Special events are held throughout the year. On Shark Day, you can watch a shark dissection. During Reptile Day, herpetologists (reptile experts) rave about these cold-blooded vertebrates. Did you know that American alligators have 80 cone-shape teeth that they lose twice a year until they stop growing? They keep the tooth fairy—or shall we say tooth mermaid—busy!

If you like this sight you may also like the National Zoo (#24).

KEEP IN MIND At the cash register where you pay for your visit, they sell Adventure Pack bags with minislides of some of the creatures. Before you consider plunking down two bucks, you might want to check out the spacious gift shop where you can purchase necklaces with shark's teeth, T-shirts, stuffed seahorses, and more.

NATIONAL ARCHIVES

Where does your family keep its most precious papers? Our nation's most important documents are housed at the National Archives. Here you can find the Declaration of Independence, the Constitution, and the Bill of Rights. If you think about it, it's rather extraordinary that our country puts these priceless papers on display to throngs of visitors who peer through protective glass for a glimpse of history. The glass is equipped with filters and filled with argon gas (it's colorless, odorless, and tasteless) to protect these irreplaceable documents from light and air, which fade and deteriorate ink and paper.

One of the most frequent questions kids ask about the National Archives concerns the 2004 award-winning movie *National Treasure,* starring Nicholas Cage. The film wasn't filmed inside the building but there are some shots of the outside of the building. In the movie, Cage's character steals the Declaration of Independence and finds a map on the backside. There isn't a map on the Declaration, but there is an upside-down note on the bottom front that reads ORIGINAL DECLARATION OF INDEPENDENCE, DATED 4TH JULY 1776. Although you can't see the flip

MAKE THE MOST OF YOUR TIME Unless you're visiting on a blistery day in February, be prepared for a line that lasts at least 30 minutes. While waiting outside, ask your child to count the Corinthian columns (there are 72). While you're waiting to see the big three documents (the Declaration, the Constitution, and the Bill of Rights), ask your child to find three famous founders in the paintings—Thomas Jefferson, Benjamin Franklin, and George Washington. For clear copies of the documents that you can read, visit the gift shop.

Constitution, between 7th and 9th Sts. NW.
Metro: Archives/Navy Memorial

 Free

Apr–Fri before Memorial Day 10–7;
Memorial Day weekend–Labor Day 10–9.
Labor Day–Mar 10–5:30

202/501–5000, www.archives.gov;
guided tours volunteer@nara.gov;
self-guided tours visitorservices@nara.gov

7 and up

side of the Declaration, other objects in the archive's vast collection that may interest kids who have studied American history include immigration records, treaties, recordings of Teddy Roosevelt's voice, and satellite maps. You can even make your own Great Seal, guess the use of a patent, and create your own documentary film.

Budding architects might notice a similarity between this building and the west wing of the National Gallery of Art (#33), the Thomas Jefferson Memorial (#13), and the DAR Constitution Hall (same address as the Dar Museum, #58). John Russell Pope designed them all in a neoclassical-revival style.

If you like this sight you might also like the National Museum of American History (#30).

KEEP IN MIND
The Declaration wasn't always stored and displayed safely behind glass at the National Archives for millions of people to view. It has had many homes, including government offices, the interiors of safes and other public displays. Wagons, ships, a Pullman sleeper, and an armored vehicle have transported this priceless document.

EATS FOR KIDS If your child is hungry for more than knowledge, the **Charters Café** sells hot and cold sandwiches, snacks, and fresh fruit. Its walls are lined with vintage agricultural posters from the archive's collection that encourage healthful eating.

NATIONAL BUILDING MUSEUM

35

The Big Bad Wolf won't blow this house down! More than 15 million bricks make up this building, designed by Civil War veteran Montgomery Meigs and constructed from 1882 to 1887. The inside of the building will awe budding builders and architects. The Great Hall, site of many inaugural balls, is 15 stories tall and is as long as a football field. Eight 75-foot Corinthian columns are among the world's largest. Though they look like marble, each is made of 70,000 bricks, covered with plaster and marbleized.

After viewing the breathtaking hall, head to the Washington: Symbol and City exhibit, where your children can handle plastic models of the Capitol, White House, Washington Monument, and Lincoln Memorial. Through interactive displays, they can create their own row houses, watch a board light up when they answer architectural questions correctly, and even choose their favorite design from among those originally submitted for the Washington Monument. Special exhibits change as often as five times per year, but all focus on the people, processes, or materials that create buildings and other "places." Recent exhibits have explored going "green" at home, and elevators, escalators, and moving sidewalks.

EATS FOR KIDS When appetites build, visit **FireHook Bakery** (tel. 202/628–0906) in the museum for hand-crafted and prepackaged sandwiches, salads, and desserts. Eat in or take your lunch to go and sit at the benches across the street at the National Law Enforcement Officers Memorial, a tribute to officers killed in duty.

MAKE THE MOST OF YOUR TIME Borrow a tool kit for $5 at the information desk. Patterns: Here, There, and Everywhere for kids 3 to 7 has stamps and rubbings and games for learning about brick patterns, Eye Spy: What Can you Find With Your Little Eye? for kids 7 to 10 includes jigsaw puzzles and create your own post-cards, and Constructor Detector for kids 8 to 11, includes a scavenger hunt and supplies to create a pattern that you can take home as a souvenir.

401 F St. NW. Metro: Judiciary Square

 Suggested donation $5

 202/272–2448; www.nbm.org

M-Sa 10–5, Su 11–5; tours
M-W 12:30, Th–Sa 11:30, 12:30,
and 1:30, Su 12:30 and 1:30

6 and up

For kids who have transitioned from tearing down towers of blocks to building their own, the Building Zone is a safe place for both. Designed for kids two to six, the Zone has a dress-up section with hard hats, tool belts, and goggles for kids who want to look like Bob the Builder. On weekends, your children (and you) can learn how bridges work and how buildings, for the most part, manage to stay in one piece.

Every day the Museum has other drop-in activities, most of which are free. And with the free Treasure Hunt (kids six and up) and Adventures in Architecture (for preteens) booklets from the Information Desk, you and your kids can explore some of the nooks and crannies of this cool building.

If you like this sight you may also like Washington National Cathedral (#5).

KEEP IN MIND Extensive school programs (also available to other groups, like scout troops) complement curricula in social studies, science, art, math, and history. Under the guidance of the museum's educators, students may plan an imaginary town, build model bridges, or assemble an 8' x 11' house from the ground up with foundations, wall frames, and trusses. Most programs cost a dollar or two for each student. For information, call the museum's education department. Check out the museum store, known as one of the best museum shops in D.C., for take-home building supplies.

NATIONAL CAPITAL TROLLEY MUSEUM

What small child doesn't love trains? And what small child who loves trains doesn't love trolleys? You can test this hypothesis at this combination trolley trip and museum. The 20-minute voyage covers 1¾ mi of track through a wooded area. Often you can spot deer, fox, rabbits, and groundhogs.

Also called streetcars, trolleys were first used in Washington, D.C., during the Lincoln administration to accommodate the influx of people during the Civil War. Early streetcars were drawn by horses, but these were replaced by cable cars and ultimately by electric cars, which skimmed quickly and smoothly along the tracks. The last Washington trolleys ran during the Kennedy administration. In fact, you might be riding in one of these last cars or in a car from another country. The museum's collection comprises 12 cars, which are all brought out on the third Sunday in April for the Cavalcade of Cars and the third Sunday in October for the Fall Open House. Both events also feature other attractions, such as a barbershop quartet or scarecrow making. During December's Holly Trolleyfest, the museum is decked in lights, and Santa greets children during the ride.

MAKE THE MOST OF YOUR TIME You can't miss the gift shop right in the middle of the museum as you enter and exit. If your child just has to have a memento, you can find a collection of Thomas the Tank Engine toys and books, plus other train-related merchandise. One thing you won't find in a toy store are trolley tickets. Each conductor uses a hole punch with a different shape—perhaps a star or zigzag. When the trolleys were in use, the holes helped identify conductors in case a passenger complained. If you're lucky, your kid won't complain about having a trolley ticket as a souvenir!

1313 Bonifant Rd., between Layhill Rd. and New Hampshire Ave., Colesville, MD

301/384–6088; www.dctrolley.org

 $4 adults, $3 children 2–17

  Jan–mid-Nov, Sa–Su 12–5; mid-Mar–mid-May and early Oct–mid-Nov, Th–F 10–2 and mid-June–mid-Aug, Th–F 11–3; Dec, Sa–Su 5–9

2–7 and all train lovers

Also take time to enjoy the museum, which resembles an old-time railroad station. Fortunately, there's no danger of losing track of your children, as the museum occupies only 1,500 square feet. With a boost, even the smallest child can press a button sending a model trolley whizzing around in a case depicting Connecticut Avenue in the early 1930s. Older kids and parents can learn the parts of a trolley and the history of D.C. trolleys through interactive computers.

Trolley memorabilia, *Thomas the Tank Engine* books, and other train-related merchandise are available in the shop. A free "Little Folks Guide to the Trolley Museum" handout and the trolley tickets themselves make nice mementos.

If you like this sight you may also like the College Park Aviation Museum (#60).

KEEP IN MIND
The biggest trolley trick for parents of toddlers is keeping them safely seated during the short ride. Luckily, the trolley makes one stop en route, when kids can get up and walk around. This is also when enthusiastic volunteers give brief trolley talks and answer questions. Often some of the passengers will remember riding the trolley when they were kids.

EATS FOR KIDS Food and drink aren't allowed in the museum or on the cars, but there are picnic tables behind the museum. Families can be choosy at the Layhill Shopping Center (Layhill and Bel Pre Rds.), where they'll find Italian fare and video games at the family-run since 1974 **Sole d' Italia** (tel. 301/598–6660), Chinese food at **Lee's Kitchen** (tel. 301/598–4810), a **McDonald's**, and a **Subway**.

NATIONAL GALLERY OF ART
AND SCULPTURE GARDEN

33

S ome kids think it looks like a bird, others a plane, but most agree it's super. Looming as large as a small aircraft, a mobile by Alexander Calder soars overhead in the East Building atrium here. It's just one of the works that fascinates kids at this art museum, one of the world's most visited. The gallery comprises two very different buildings and a sculpture garden. The airy and spacious East Building's modern art—by Picasso, Matisse, Miró, and others—appeals to children, as does the exterior of the I. M. Pei–designed trapezoidal structure. In fact, since its 1978 opening, the bladelike southwest corner has been darkened and polished smooth by thousands of hands irresistibly drawn to touch it.

In the neoclassical West Building, more than 100 galleries contain 13th- to 19th-century works. Though art lovers easily spend all day here, most little children last about an hour. (Strollers are available at both buildings' entrances.) Students of architecture may notice that the building's dome shape resembles the Jefferson Memorial. Both buildings were designed by John Russell Pope and opened in the early 1940s.

KEEP IN MIND When it's too cold to enjoy the sculpture garden, toddlers might enjoy the moving walkway in the underground tunnel connecting the East and West buildings. But for older kids in the winter, there's more to do here than see artwork. Ice-skating is offered mid-March through mid-November, weather permitting.

MAKE THE MOST OF YOUR TIME Free weekend Family Workshops (registration required; call up to 3 weeks in advance) include tours and activities. If you'd rather go it alone, start in the Information Room in the West Building to preview works by computer. Or you may rent the Adventures in Art family audio tour, which explores Dutch and Flemish paintings ($3 per tour, $2 for extra headphones, ages 7–12).

4th St. and Constitution Ave. NW, East Building; 6th and Constitution, NW, West Building. Metro: Judiciary Square, Archives, Smithsonian

 Free

M–Sa 10–5, Su 11–6

 202/737–4215, 202/842–6176 TDD; www.nga.gov/kids

4 and up

Even the littlest tots enjoy the sculpture garden. The massive *Spider* by Louise Bourgeois is large enough to frighten even the bravest Miss Muffet. The rabbit *Thinker on a Rock,* by Barry Flanagan can promote a discussion about other famous rabbits. Ask your child, "What do you suppose it's thinking about?" The only sculpture kids (or adults) can touch is Scott Burton's *Six-Part Seating,* with its polished granite chairs. Still, the meandering paths reveal unexpected treasures, such as Roy Lichtenstein's *House I.* Claes Oldenburg and Coosje van Bruggen's mammoth *Typewriter Eraser, Scale X* will look foreign to kids born in the computer age. Ask your kids to guess what it is.

If your family likes this sight they may also like the Phillips Collection (#20).

EATS FOR KIDS The gallery offers several options: **On the Concourse,** a buffet, serves pizza, sandwiches, chicken strips, and more. The **Espresso Bar** sells freshly made gelato and sobetto as well as specialty sweets. In the West Building, the **Garden Café** (tel. 202/712–7460; reservations recommended for groups of more than eight) features American fare. On Sunday (11–3), try the jazz brunch in the East Building's **Terrace Café**, which overlooks the Mall and the huge Calder mobile. Or, pick up a pizza or a sandwich outside at the sculpture garden's **Pavilion Café**.

NATIONAL GEOGRAPHIC
MUSEUM AT EXPLORERS HALL

The National Geographic Society's famous yellow-bordered magazine—found in doctors' offices, family rooms, and attics nationwide—is not exactly for kids. Yet Explorers Hall brings the planet's wonders closer and shows kids that it is indeed a small world after all.

Exhibits rotate here just as the moon and Earth do. Displays vary, just like the magazine's features. Dinosaurs, glowing worms and mutant fireflies, modern mapping with a 10-foot globe, the *March of the Penguins* movie with a live appearance from these live flightless birds, and King Tut's mummified remains have all been studied in depth here. One exhibit about what scientists have learned from "Crittercams" (data-collecting devices worn by the animals) had kids crawl though a tunnel and pop up in a bubble to come face-to-face with a penguin wearing a working Crittercam.

Kids can ham it up and see their faces on the cover of the *National Geographic*. Postcard-size pictures ($5) can be made at In the Picture, where they can choose their own

MAKE THE MOST OF YOUR TIME
The good news is that the exhibits here are well-researched, very visual, modern, and when they're for families, very fun. The bad news is that there's a chance that the current exhibits might not be appropriate for all ages. Exhibits change about every three to six months.

EATS FOR KIDS
In a neighborhood catering to businesspeople, you won't find high chairs, but you will find reasonable prices. In addition to a **Quiznos**, **Potbelly**, and **Subway** nearby, the self-service **California Grill** (1720 M St. NW, tel. 202/463–4200) specializes in Mexican and American cuisine and the **Mudd House** (1724 M St. NW, tel. 202/822–8455) offers a place for parents to sip specialty coffees while kids warm up with hot chocolate.

1145 17th St. NW. Metro: Farragut North, Farragut West

 Free

202/857-7588; www.ngmuseum.org

M–Sa 9–5, Su 10–5

5 and up

backgrounds—among 12 scenes such as tulips outside the White House, the Great Wall of China, Mount Everest, or even the moon. Other props include furry creatures like panda bears, tigers, or gorillas.

365 days of the year, 24 hours a day, you can walk outside the museum's portico and peer through the glass to see relief maps created with satellite imagery and artifacts from past expeditions. You may watch and listen to the National Geographic channel or check out the electronic ticker tape, which, not unexpectedly, tells about the latest expeditions, adventures, and discoveries in science and geography.

If you like this sight you may also like the Newseum (#23).

KEEP IN MIND Through magazines, TV, radio, maps, books, CD-ROMs, and the Internet, the National Geographic Society brings the world of geography to more than 300 million people worldwide. You can find many of the Society's publications in the gift shop, including *National Geographic Kids*, a magazine for 6 to 14-year-olds.

NATIONAL MUSEUM OF AFRICAN ART

Kids can really relate to the art at this museum. Perhaps it's because every child has turned a paper plate into a mask or strung beads together to make a necklace. Perhaps it's because so many of the works incorporate animals. Wander through this Smithsonian museum with your child, and you can see all sorts of African artworks: musical instruments, pottery, beaded works, sculptures, carvings, and masks and headdresses made to entertain or personify characters or animals. Jewelry on display is made of such materials as beads, woods, fiber, bronze, ivory, and fired clay.

One of the best ways to learn about the arts and cultures of Africa is through the AfriKid Art programs, aimed at kids 4 and up. At drop-in workshops (most of which are free), children are taught about the materials, colors, animals, and countries of origin of items in the permanent collection, such as a colorful beaded crown or a life-size figure of a man. They may also be asked to answer questions like, "How would you describe the object to someone who couldn't see it?" or "How do you think it would feel to wear this hat?" After

MAKE THE MOST OF YOUR TIME To expand your children's global view even further, walk about 100 paces west through the Enid A. Haupt Garden or just open the door at the end of the Art of the Personal Object gallery, and you'll be in the Sackler Gallery (*see #17*), which is connected to the Freer Gallery of Art. The emphasis at these nearby museums is on another continent altogether: Asia.

950 Independence Ave. SW.
Metro: Smithsonian

202/633-1000, 202/357-1729 TTY;
www.nmafa.si.edu

 Free

 Daily 10–5:30

4 and up

touring the gallery, kids pursue an activity, such as beading, weaving, or hat making, and can take their masterpiece home as a souvenir.

To help in your exploration, consider counting the number of masks or musical instruments in the gallery.

The museum also has storytelling sessions, during which folktales are often combined with music and dance to bring legends from the African continent to life. And in the true tradition of African storytelling, the audience frequently chimes in.

If you like this sight you may also like the National Museum of Women in the Arts (#26).

KEEP IN MIND The gift shop, like all Smithsonian stores, doesn't charge any sales tax. Chances are you'll see some cool items here, including animals made from beads, wood, and even old soda cans. You might even find chocolate bars from Ghana.

EATS FOR KIDS Pick up fresh fruit, bread, and more on Friday from June through September at the Farmers' Market in the parking lot outside the Department of Agriculture (12th St. and Independence Ave.). Check out the food at the National Air and Space Museum (#39), the National Museum of Natural History (#27), the National Museum of the American Indian (#29), and the National Museum of American History (#30), which all have on-site restaurants.

NATIONAL MUSEUM OF
AMERICAN HISTORY

20

Oh say, can you see the flag that inspired "The Star-Spangled Banner," Oscar the Grouch, an original teddy bear from 1903, first ladies' inaugural gowns, and a five-story dollhouse? You can, and you can see lots more American memorabilia on three floors of exhibitions, whose incredible diversity of artifacts gave it the nickname "the nation's attic," but this phrase no longer fits. After an $85 million renovation, this museum is as well organized as if it were new.

If you're with train-loving tots, head to the first floor to see the big rigs. Exhibits on the first floor emphasize the history of science and technology and include farm machines, antique automobiles, and a 260-ton steam locomotive. America on the Move starts in 1856 as the railroad comes to a California town and ends in 1999 in Los Angeles, the "Ellis Island of the end of the 20th century" as pilgrims arrive from other countries daily. Maybe your children will follow the 14 historical settings in chronological order, but chances are they'll zip through, pointing out the 1939 Dodge school bus painted "double deep"

MAKE THE MOST OF YOUR TIME During busy times, the Hands-On Science Center requires passes, which let you stay ½ hour. The free passes are available on a first-come, first-served basis at the door. Adults must accompany children in this room.

EATS FOR KIDS If your kids scream for ice cream, visit the museum's **café and gelato bar** (first floor, Constitution Avenue entrance) for an Italian treat. For more options, the **Main Street Café** on the lower level serves all-American barbeque, pizza, sandwiches, burgers, salads and dessert. When the weather is good, grab a hot dog from the food carts and picnic outside.

14th St. and Constitution Ave. NW.
Metro: Smithsonian, Federal Triangle

 Free

202/633-1000;
www.americanhistory.si.edu

Daily 10–5:30; Hands-On Science T–F
12:30–5, Sa–Su 10–5. Reopens after
renovation summer 2008

2 and up, Hands-On
Science 5 and up

orange; the toy ride-in car; and the 1955 station wagon with wood paneling. Look for "Bud," the official mascot of the exhibit, and his signs designed to stimulate family discussion about the exhibit. Two *Jurassic Park* eggs and an orange-masked Teenage Mutant Ninja Turtle are in the Science in American Life exhibit on the first floor.

The second floor, devoted to U.S. social and political history, even contains a house. Within These Walls follows the lives of families who lived at 16 Elm Street in Ipswich, Massachusetts, from the mid-1760s through 1945. The third floor's Icons of American Pop Culture displays familiar items, including Dorothy's ruby slippers from *The Wizard of Oz*. For a more interactive visit, children and adults should stop at the Hands-On Science Center. Kids, unravel the mysteries of DNA, conduct tests for water pollutants as scientists did in the 1880s, and become "Star-Spangled Banner" conservators.

If you like this sight you may also like the National Museum of Women in the Arts (#26).

KEEP IN MIND This museum is a great way to bring American history to life for kids of all ages. In The American Presidency: A Glorious Burden, you can see the portable wooden lap desk that Thomas Jefferson designed and used to draft the Declaration of Independence. Also check out George Washington's sword and Abraham Lincoln's top hat.

NATIONAL MUSEUM OF
THE AMERICAN INDIAN

Your introduction to American Indian life and indeed U.S. history begins before you enter this Smithsonian museum that opened in 2004. Plants that were native to the area before European settlers arrived grow in an upland hardwood forest, lowland freshwater wetlands, and a meadow. Crops known as the "three sisters"—corn, beans, and squash—will also grow. Cascading water represents purification and a nurturing spirit. Even the building's stone-clad forms reflect the wearing by wind and water over time.

Above the information desk, look and listen as the words and sounds at the Welcome Wall come from languages of Native people from the northern tip of the Arctic to the southern tip of South America. Then feel the cool copper bands woven into the wall representing traditions of textiles and basketry. No matter when you arrive, look at the "light show" reflected from the prism window. When the sun is at its peak, from 11 AM to 2 PM, the sun's beams dance across the floors and walls.

KEEP IN MIND The two museum stores carry an impressive collection of books for children about Native American life, from the lovely legends of yesteryear to life today to folklore fantasies. In *Coyote in Love with a Star*, the famous trickster takes a job as a rodent control officer at the former World Trade Center in New York City. Through the *My World* book series, kids meet real Native American children. You can also pick up some authentic native crafts here at reasonable prices. But a better reminder of your visit is free. Send a souvenir e-mail postcard home by visiting the resource center on the third floor.

4th St. and Independence Ave. SW.
Metro: Federal Center SW/L'Enfant Plaza,
Maryland Ave. exit

 202/633-1000;
www.AmericanIndian.si.edu

 Free

Daily 10–5:30

2 and up

Check out the floor-to-ceiling cases along the walls of the Window on Collections' exhibits. Challenge your child to find the walrus head made out of motorcycle parts and the toy buffalo made from the hide of these massive beasts.

The museum also helps explore old cultural myths. You've heard of cowboys and Indians. Well, some Native Americans were and are cowboys and cowgirls, too. They still ranch and entertain folks with their rodeo skills. Even children who have studied American Indians may be surprised to learn that more died from diseases brought from European settlers than from wars.

Kids too young to appreciate history will enjoy the sights and sounds of Native bead workers, weavers, drummers, storytellers, and dancers at the museum's indoor and outdoor theaters.

If you like this sight you may also like the planetarium shows at Rock Creek Park (#19).

EATS FOR KIDS Watch salmon being cooked over a fire pit built into the floor of the museum's **Mitsitam Native Foods Café.** Mitsitam means "Let's Eat" in the language of the Delaware and Piscataway. If your kids do not care for salmon, they probably like turkey. Choose from food native to five geographic regions: Northern Woodlands, South America, Northwest Coast, Meso-American, and the Great Plains. Whatever region's cuisine you select, try to get a seat at the window where it looks as if the water outside disappears under your feet.

MAKE THE MOST OF YOUR TIME

Who We Are, a 3-minute presentation on the fourth floor, is a great introduction to contemporary Native life, but if your child covers her ears during thunderstorms, it might be wise to skip it.

NATIONAL MUSEUM OF HEALTH AND MEDICINE

Boys and girls who want real goose bumps or who have an interest in a medical career can find lots of really cool stuff at this medical museum that depicts the fight against injury and disease. Because some of the exhibits are fairly graphic (e.g., wax surgical models, organs in formaldehyde), the museum may be unsuitable for the squeamish.

At the Human Body exhibit, kids explore how the body works, in sickness and in health. They can get an up-close look at human organs, like livers, stomachs, lungs, and kidneys. Compare a smoker's lung to a coal miner's lung, view a brain still attached to a spinal cord, and see the mega-colon. Some organs are "plastinated"—preserved in plastic so they can be touched—and injected with blue and red dyes so arteries can be distinguished from veins. All are real.

KEEP IN MIND There's a fear factor here. My sons, who were 12 and 14, thought the exhibits were "nasty, disgusting, and repulsive." I was a bit grossed out, too, but I was also secretly thrilled: I knew our trip had made an impression.

This place is full of bizarre stuff and stories. During the Battle of Gettysburg, a 12-pound cannonball splintered the right leg of Civil War General Daniel E. Sickles. After it was

MAKE THE MOST OF YOUR TIME Docents lead tours of the museum on the second and fourth Saturday of every month at 1. Tours last 1–1½ hours and are recommended for ages 11 and up. Most docents focus on Civil War medicine. If you call ahead, the docents will bring out plastinated organs for you to feel. To keep *your* organs healthy, many docents share a tip unknown to Civil War physicians, who spread a lot of germs: wash your hands.

6900 Georgia Ave. NW, campus of Walter Reed
Army Medical Center (off Elder St.)

 Free

 202/782-2200;
www.nmhm.washingtondc.museum

Daily 10–5:30

9 and up

amputated, he sent the leg to this museum, then known as the Army Medical Museum, where it's still on display, along with a picture of the general as an amputee. Incidentally, the eccentric General Sickles used to visit his leg here and would sometimes bring friends to see it.

At other exhibits, your children can learn about the evolution of the microscope, view the human body from a 3-D perspective, look at early medical instruments used in skull surgery, and discover why disease killed more soldiers than bullets during the Civil War. The most famous object on display is the bullet that killed President Lincoln at Ford's Theatre (#54). There's much here to make everyone grateful for modern medicine. Take a look at the leeches, used centuries ago to treat diseases. Actually, some hospitals still use them.

If you like this sight you may also like the United States Botanic Garden (#12) with its medicinal plants.

EATS FOR KIDS For great selection and low prices, walk to the **Walter Reed Hospital Cafeteria** (Bldg. 2, tel. 202/782-2027). Or select a sandwich from **Subway** (also in Bldg. 2). **Burger King** is in building 1. Or drive a mile and a half for seafood at **Crisfield** (8012 Georgia Ave., Silver Spring, tel. 301/589-1306) served in a casual atmosphere with swivel chairs for teens and booster seats for little ones.

NATIONAL MUSEUM OF NATURAL HISTORY

S ay hello to Henry. One of the largest elephants ever found in the world, this stuffed beast has greeted generations of kids in the rotunda of this huge museum, which is dedicated to natural wonders of the world, both big and small.

In the popular Dinosaur Hall, fossilized skeletons range from a 90-foot-long diplodocus to a tiny *Thesalorsaurus neglectus* (so named because its bones sat for years in a museum drawer before being reassembled). Cross the Rotunda (from the Dinosaur Hall) to the Hall of Mammals that features 274 creatures, including lions and tigers and bears, plus more exotic animals from the Australian tree kangaroos to a South American fairy armadillo, but the star of the exhibit is a little tiny shrewlike creature, nicknamed "Morgie" for *Morganucodon oehleri*, one of the Earth's first mammals. Four-inch long Morgie forged for food with dinosaurs 210 million years ago. A bronze sculpture depicts a slightly enlarged Morgie that is developing a shiny coat as kids pet their ancient ancestor.

MAKE THE MOST OF YOUR TIME Children explore with their hands in the Discovery Room. In the Discovery Center, you'll find the 487-seat Samuel C. Johnson Theater and its IMAX films. For 3-D flicks, you get to don oversize glasses. You won't need glasses to see the Dinosaur Hall's triceratops, on the first floor. Scientists studied this massive herbivore (plant eater) by scanning bones and using computers to make a life-like cast and video. Kids can compare it to what scientists in 1905 thought the triceratops looked like.

Constitution Ave. and 10th St. NW.
Metro: Smithsonian

 Free

Daily 10–5:30; Discovery Room T–F 12–2:30, Sa–Su
10:30–3:30; Memorial Day–Labor Day, T–Su 10:30–30
(free passes may be required on busy days)

202/633–1000, 202/357–1729 TTY;
www.mnh.si.edu

 2 and up, Discovery Room

Older children may enjoy the Janet Annenberg Hooker Hall of Geology, Gems & Minerals, which takes rock collecting to new heights and includes a neat exhibit on volcanoes and earthquakes. The Hope Diamond is also here, slowly rotating in a four-sided glass case. The most-visited museum object in the world, it's even more popular than the *Mona Lisa*.

Not everything in the museum is dead or inanimate, though. For some action, take your kids to the second floor's O. Orkin Insect Zoo, home to live ants, bees, centipedes, tarantulas, roaches—some as large as mice, and other critters you wouldn't want in your house. After viewing these creepy creatures, young bug fanciers can act the part by crawling through a model of an African termite mound.

If you like this sight you may also like the National Zoo (#24).

KEEP IN MIND
In the Insect Zoo, roaches that freak out people are behind glass, but in the Butterfly Pavillion, winged insects freely fly overhead.

EATS FOR KIDS Tarantula feedings usually take place in the Insect Zoo at 10:30, 11:30, and 1:30 Tuesday through Friday and 11:30, 12:30, and 1:30 on weekends. Whereas the tarantulas' meal plan consists of the same old thing every day (crickets), you have lots of choices in the museum's 600-seat **Atrium Café** and the **Fossil Café**, where you eat at tables with little fossilized artifacts and illustrations under glass.

NATIONAL MUSEUM OF
WOMEN IN THE ARTS

Every day is International Women's Day at this beautifully restored 1908 Renaissance Revival building, showcasing works by prominent female artists from the Renaissance to the present. Ironically, it was once a men-only Masonic temple. Today, in addition to traveling shows, the museum houses a permanent collection, including paintings, drawings, sculpture, prints, and photographs by such artists as Mary Cassatt, Frida Kahlo, Gabrielle Münter, and Helen Frankenthaler.

As at many art museums, it's not easy to know what children will like. Frida Baranek's nonobjective sculpture keeps kids talking. Some youngsters think this untitled work looks like a bird's nest or a huge tumbleweed that moves, albeit subtly. Others say it reminds them of a bad-hair day. Nineteenth-century French artist Rosa Bonheur is known for imaginative animal paintings, filled with rich and realistic textures. Teens may enjoy contrasting their practical clothes (some more practical than others) with the ornate Renaissance-era clothing of the young woman in Lavinia Fontana's *Portrait of a Noblewoman* (1580).

EATS FOR KIDS Macaroni n' cheese, crispy chicken, and meat loaf are part of the draw at the **Capitol City Brewing Company** (1100 New York Ave. NW, tel. 202/628–2222). For the more adventurous eater, **Haad Thai** (1100 New York Ave. NW, tel. 202/682–1111) offers kids crispy rolls and chicken on a skewer.

MAKE THE MOST OF YOUR TIME Once a year, the museum is transformed from formal to fun as women and men, girls and boys gather here for music, dancing, hands-on crafts, storytelling, and more at the museum's annual Family Festival. Usually celebrating another culture, the event is generally held in early spring, but the date varies because the festival is tied in with special exhibits. By October, the museum staff should be able to tell you when the next Family Festival will be held.

1250 New York Ave. NW.
Metro: Metro Center

 $5 adults 19 and up, $3 students 19 and up; some exhibits extra. The first Sunday of the month is free admission.

 M–Sa 10–5, Su 12–5

202/783–5000;
www.nmwa.org

6 and up

Free family programs for children and role-model workshops for teens are held about once a month. Reservations are required for most programs. If you're not attending a children's program, stop by the Education Gallery to learn more about special exhibits and works from the permanent collection. From early June through mid-September, you can see artwork created by kids who participate in the museum's Bridging Communities program. To find out how the kids made such cool masterpieces, watch the short video of them at work.

At the information desk, pick up an "Artventure" brochure (ages 6–10), which suggests ways to look at art through the elements of line, shape, color, and texture. Even though the artists covered at the museum are limited to women, the approach to art and the appeal to visitors are universal.

If you like this sight you may also like the Corcoran Gallery of Art (#59), the city's oldest art museum.

KEEP IN MIND It's hard for many kids to understand why it's significant to have a museum that only displays art by women. Here's one idea to get your child interested in the art here: Ask about bugs. When Maria Sibylla Merian (born 1647) was about 14 years old, she started collecting, studying, and drawing insects. You can see Maria Merian's highly descriptive etchings and watercolors at the museum.

Look up and see one of the first airmail planes. Look down and see floor tiles shaped like stamped envelopes. Look around and you can see first-class opportunities for children at this Smithsonian-operated museum dedicated to the history of our mail service and stamps.

Transportation-loving tots can pretend to move a lot of mail here. They can steer and push dozens of buttons on a full-size, big-rig truck cab right in the corner of the main exhibit area. Then they can experience what it was like to walk through the woods on route in the Binding the Nation exhibit by following a Native American trail that postal carriers followed between New York and Boston. There aren't any signs to guide you. The only way to find the right route is to look for notches in the trees.

Holograms, computer games, and interactive devices highlight the exhibit What's in the Mail for You? The best way to start in this exhibit is with a mirror station; three are placed at eye level for people of all heights. Below the mirrors, kids can type information and

MAKE THE MOST OF YOUR TIME This Smithsonian museum is much smaller than its cousins on the Mall. You can wander through in about 45 minutes. Call or ask about activities in the Discovery Center, near the statue of Ben Franklin, the first U.S. postmaster. Kids may play games, hear stories, and create crafts that reflect museum exhibits. For example, in March kids might study an Irish immigration stamp and make shamrock wands. In April they often create hats to wear for Earth Day, and June might see them making flags to celebrate Flag Day. Come early for the best selection of materials.

2 Massachusetts Ave. NE.
Metro: Union Station

 Free

 Daily 10–5:30

202/633-5555 recording, 202/633-1000 voice,
202/633-9849 TTY; www.postalmuseum.si.edu

3 and up

push buttons on screens to answer questions about everything from where they live to what kinds of music and television shows they enjoy. Plastic profile cards, shaped like credit cards, help teach how direct marketers target their mailings.

In addition to all of the neat stuff here, the museum houses a collection of stamps. By pulling handles on vertical glass files, you can see foreign stamps organized by country, and U.S. stamps organized by date, from 5- and 10-cent stamps of 1847 to the latest issues. When you're ready to leave the museum, make sure your children check out the customized postcard machine. After a postcard is addressed, the computer uses maps and sound to show how it will travel to its intended destination.

If you like this sight you may also like the National Geographic Museum at Explorers Hall (#32).

EATS FOR KIDS Gettysburger Address (cheeseburger) and Federal (chicken) Fingers are on the kids' menu at the **Capitol City Brewing Company** (2 Massachusetts Ave. NE, tel. 202/842–2337), in the same building as the museum. Across the street, you can find restaurants and more than 35 food stands offering everything from pizza to sushi at **Union Station** (50 Massachusetts Ave. NE). One of the best eateries is **America** (*see* D.C. Ducks, #57), with suitably American regional fare. **Johnny Rockets** (tel. 202/289–6969), a 1950s-style hamburger joint, also appeals to families.

KEEP IN MIND
While this museum helps give kids an appreciation for the postal system, they might like to know that camels, birds, reindeer, and dogs have all helped deliver the mail. Although Owney the Dog never carried any, he was still the mascot of the railway mail service in the late 19th century. Thanks to taxidermy, you can actually see Owney at the museum.

NATIONAL ZOO

Known more for political animals than real animals, Washington nevertheless possesses one of the world's foremost zoos. Start with any must-see creatures on your child's list. On busy days there may be waits at the popular animal houses, such as the Giant Panda House, Reptile Discovery Center, or Amazonia's tropical rain forest. In the Flight Room, birds fly unrestricted. Orangutans swing on overhead cables from the Great Ape House to the Think Tank, where you can get a good look at the big apes while they get a better look at you. High-tech orangutans communicate with researchers using touch-screen computers.

Set among waterfalls, rocks, and bamboo grooves, the Asia Trail opened in 2006 as the home to red pandas, Asian small-clawed otters, sloth bears, clouded leopards and the zoo's most popular residents. Adoring fans flock to the new panda pair, who arrived in 2001 after years of negotiations with China. This playful, high-profile couple, named Tian Tian (pronounced t-YEN t-YEN and meaning "more and more") and Mei Xiang (roughly pronounced may shong and meaning "beautiful fragrance"), lives in the original

KEEP IN MIND A trip to the zoo makes for an exhausting but fulfilling day. So that everyone emerges happy and healthy, pace yourselves; don't rush around trying to see everything. You can't. And watch your kids carefully; the biggest safety problem here is not animals but children wandering off.

MAKE THE MOST OF YOUR TIME The Cleveland Park Metro stop is a better choice than Woodley Park/Zoo, with an uphill walk to the zoo but a downhill walk when you leave. Rental strollers are available. Parking lots fill up in summer, so arrive early. In summer, early morning (or late afternoon) is a better time to catch animals alert; in cooler months, they're more active at midday. Also: If you visit the zoo more than four days a year, consider a FONZ (Friends of the National Zoo) membership.

3001 Connecticut Ave. NW.
Metro: Cleveland Park, Woodley Park/Zoo

 Free

Daylight saving time: grounds daily 6 AM–8 PM,
animal buildings 10–6; Standard time: grounds
daily 6–6, animal buildings 10–4:30.

 202/633–4800 or 202/673–0127;
www.nationalzoo.si.edu

 All ages

pandas' renovated habitat. On July 9, 2005, Mei Xiang gave birth to a little male cub, Tai Shan (pronounced tie-SHON and meaning "peaceful mountain"). In keeping with Chinese tradition, the cub was named 100 days after its birth. If your kid usually has his ears plugged with an MP3 player, he or she can go to the zoo's Web site and download an audio tour to use on the Asia trail.

To see the world's fastest feline, check out the Cheetah Conservation area. To see animals with anywhere from zero to eight legs, visit the invertebrate exhibit, where octopuses, nautiluses, and giant spiders dwell. For barking and clapping, visit the sea lions at 11:30 in Beaver Valley. If your child's idea of animals relates to lyrics with the letters E-I-E-I-O, check out the new Kids' Farm where you'll not only see animals that moo, neigh, cluck, and oink, you might get to help the zoo groom goats and miniature donkeys.

If you like this sight you may also like the National Aquarium (#37).

EATS FOR KIDS At the pizza playground next to the Kid's Farm, children can jump around on a huge rubber-surfaced pizza. When your tummies start to growl for a real bite to eat, check out the food kiosks, the **Mane Restaurant** on Lion/Tiger Hill or the **Panda Café,** near—what else—the Giant Panda House. Both restaurants serve a variety of kid-friendly food.

NEWSEUM

What is news? At this $450 million, 250,000-square-foot high-tech museum (as of press time, slated to open in early 2008), you and your children can experience the story behind the headlines and even make some news of your own. Primarily funded by the Freedom Forum, a nonpartisan foundation dedicated to free press and free speech, this facility is a showcase for how and why news is made.

This facility replaced the Newseum in Arlington, Virginia, which opened in 1997 and drew 2.25 million visitors in its five-year history. In this location the Newseum hopes to attract many more people. It certainly offers more, including 15 theaters, two high-definition television studios, touch-screen timelines, and more to tell the story of the news—not only of today but also of yesterday and tomorrow.

Put your knowledge of the news into action. Through the use of computers, your kids can experience what it's like to be a reporter or editor. They'll contemplate the ethics of anonymous

MAKE THE MOST OF YOUR TIME Admission to the 4-D movie in the Annenberg Theater is free, but you need to pick up timed-entry tickets at the information desk. In less than 20 minutes, this flick covers three journalists in three centuries: Isaiah Thomas reporting on the Battle of Lexington, reporter Nellie Bly going under cover at a mental institution, and broadcaster Edward R. Murrow reporting on the German blitz of London.

555 Pennsylvania Ave. NW.
Metro: Judiciary Square or Archives

 $17.91; $13 ages 7–12, under 7 free

 Daily 9–5

202/292-6397 or 888/639-7386;
www.newseum.org

7 and up

sources and bias. Some questions may transfer to the lives of preteens and teens. For example as a reporter, you find out that your neighbor has been arrested. Do you tell your editor?

Or your kids might like to appear on camera, reading the news from a monitor in front of videos of the White House, the National Zoo, or the weather. For $5, they can perform for visitors in the Newseum and transmit their segments via the Web.

Journalists are known for asking poignant questions and listening. After visiting this museum of news, you might find that your child will have a lot to talk about.

If you like this site, you might also like the International Spy Museum (#47).

KEEP IN MIND Because a lot of news concerns war and death, some exhibits in the Newseum may be perplexing or inappropriate for young children. You can't necessarily predict when you'll come upon a graphic image, and screens constantly display today's news. It's best to provide guidance throughout the museum if your child is under 10 or is particularly sensitive.

EATS FOR KIDS For a bite without leaving the building, try the **Food Section** on the concourse level. The cafeteria seats 152. But if you'd rather treat your future Katie Couric or John Stewart to a more formal meal try the **Source by Wolfgang Puck**. On the street level, the Source is a grill but upstairs it's fine dining.

OXON COVE PARK

If you want to take your children back to an era when taking care of the animals meant more than walking the family dog or feeding the cat, visit this working farm (also called Oxon Hill Farm) administered by the National Park Service. On a site where the Piscataway Indians once lived, this farm has animals and equipment typical of life in a bygone era—mostly the early 19th century and later.

Down on this farm you can find draft horses, sheep, pigs, ducks, geese, turkeys, cows, and goats—known as poor man's cows because they're capable of eating about anything and still producing milk and cheese. Many children's favorite animal is Tuesday, the milk cow, who because she was previously a show cow doesn't have horns. Unlike in the 19th century, most modern farmers stunt the growth of horns, as they're a hazard to farmers and other cows and they're no longer needed for protection.

KEEP IN MIND People often think that pigs are dumb, but some farmers believe they learn more quickly than horses and dogs. One popular conception that does hold true, however, concerns their trough manners. Watch as the cows' milk is delivered to them. Then ask your kids if they like pigs!

MAKE THE MOST OF YOUR TIME The farm gets the most visitors during the spring and fall when school groups come, but there's always parking and plenty of room for everyone to explore. Whenever you visit, remind your children to move slowly near the animals and not to make any loud noises or sudden motions. Such actions are likely to startle them. And though you will no doubt get a kick out of watching your child getting a kick out of the animals, also take a moment to appreciate the panoramic view of Washington over the Potomac River.

6411 Oxon Hill Rd., Oxon Hill, MD

 Free

 301/839-1176; www.nps.gov/oxhi

Daily 8–4:30

1–11

With supervision, your children can milk a cow, collect eggs warm from the nest, and—if raccoons haven't eaten it—crack and shell corn to feed the chickens. Hayrides depart afternoons at 1:30, except on Friday when they leave at 11.

A furnished parlor in a white farmhouse owned by the DeButts family in the early 1800s is open a few times each week. Park rangers and volunteers are usually on hand to talk about the British-born Mrs. DeButts and her views on slavery and the War of 1812. Call ahead to find out when kids can participate in daily chores and when the farmhouse is open. Free, farm-fresh programs, including sheep shearing in May, cider making in September, corn harvesting in October, and Talking Turkey in November are also available. Junior Ranger programs in the summertime teach 9- to 12-year-olds about farm life. Reservations for all programs are a must.

If you like this sight you may also like the Kids' Farm at the National Zoo (#24).

EATS FOR KIDS For fresh food, bring your own and take advantage of picnic tables in the shade near the parking lot, along the path to the farm, or near the house. Otherwise, your options consist of **fast-food outlets** along Oxon Hill Road and the **Outback Steakhouse** (6091 Oxon Hill Rd., tel. 301/839–4300), a few miles away. Here kids can color and do crossword puzzles while they eat (or maybe so you can eat!).

PATUXENT NATIONAL WILDLIFE
VISITOR CENTER

W hat kind of noise does a blue jay make? How does a katydid sound? What about a beaver? Your kids are bound to find out: The first stop at the Patuxent Research Refuge is the Nature Calls kiosk. No spelling, reading, or typing is required to learn about the refuge's animals at this animated game in the lobby. But that's just the beginning as kids track down animals inside and outside this huge modern nature center.

Older kids might want to hang around Nature Calls to set up a rap session for birds, while younger kids may want to skip ahead to view Handles on Habitat, where they can pull a knob to see a pelican and osprey appear in the Chesapeake Bay or push a button to watch a scientist pop up with a mirror to look at birds' nests in the Hawaiian rain forest. Life-size dioramas of wild animals depict whooping cranes, timber wolves, and California sea otters swimming in kelp. The exhibits have enough buttons and knobs to amuse even toddlers.

EATS FOR KIDS Although picnicking is not allowed, on a pleasant day you may bring snacks to eat on the visitor center patio. Otherwise, the staff at the front desk can direct you to local **fast-food restaurants**, many of which are along Route 197. A 15-minute drive away in Laurel, **Pasta Plus** (209 Gorman Ave., tel. 301/498–5100) serves up home-made pastas, breads, and desserts, which you can also carry out.

10901 Scarlet Tanager Loop (off Powder Mill Rd., between Rte. 197 and Baltimore-Washington Pkwy.), Laurel, MD

 Free, tram $3 ages 13 and up, $1 children 3–12

Daily 9–4:30; tram mid-Mar–mid-Nov, Sa–Su 11:30–3

301/497-5763; patuxent.fws.gov

 2 and up

Patuxent hosts hunts, hikes, and activities for naturalists of all ages throughout the year. For example, preschoolers are advised to "dress to get dirty" for Whacky Wetlands. Dragonflies of Patuxent is designed for kids 12-plus to learn how to identify these ferocious predators of the pond. The Kids Fishing Day held in early June, attracts hundreds of anglers hoping for the big one.

You can take your own wildlife tour by following the well-marked trails. The paved Wildlife Loop is wide enough for a double stroller but short enough (about ⅓ mi) so preschoolers won't wear out. At the bird-viewing blind, even the youngest kids (with a boost from you) can peer through a slat as birds swoop within a few inches of their faces. About another 4 mi of trails, made of wood chips and other natural materials, satisfy junior and senior naturalists.

If you like this sight you may also like Rock Creek Park (#19).

MAKE THE MOST OF YOUR TIME

On spring and fall weekends and daily through the summer, a 35-minute narrated tram tour runs through the refuge's meadows, forests, and wetlands, weather permitting. Though the narrator's commentary about wildlife management may be too advanced for your children, they probably will find the ride thrilling enough.

KEEP IN MIND You may be tempted to leave most of your cash at home since, with the exception of the tram ride, all activities are free. However, bring a little money for the Wildlife Images Bookstore, which sells some interesting children's merchandise at reasonable prices. Your children might like some stickers, rubber creatures, posters, or playing cards with pictures of endangered animals on them. Profits benefit the refuge.

PHILLIPS COLLECTION

This kid-comfortable museum, where you can sit back on a puffy couch or plop down on the carpet, was once the home—albeit the grand one—of Duncan Phillips, founder of the museum. In this home and in similarly scaled additions that retain the intimacy of a private residence, the museum features impressionists and modern American and European art. Six fireplaces and one fake fireplace (which looks real) add to the museum's homey feel. Unlike most other galleries, where uniformed guards appear uninterested in the masterpieces around them, the Phillips employs art students, many of whom are artists themselves, to sit by the paintings and answer questions.

The collection's best-known painting, Pierre-Auguste Renoir's *Luncheon of the Boating Party,* is particularly interesting to children because of its bright colors, the people engaged in happy conversation, and the terrier on the table. Kids can also relate to subjects like a ballet rehearsal, by Edgar Degas; a bullfight, by Pablo Picasso; and children playing hide-and-seek in a 19th-century house, by William Merritt Chase. Works by Swiss painter

KEEP IN MIND The Phillips Collection staff requests that everyone turn off their cell phones in the gallery. Also, keep a safe distance—12 inches—from all paintings and sculpture, because artwork can be damaged by accident.

EATS FOR KIDS Purchase sandwiches, salads, and pastries at the **Firehook Bakery and Coffee House** (tel. 202/387–2151 Ext. 351) in the gallery overlooking a courtyard. Open 10–4 Tuesday through Saturday and from 11 to 4 on Sunday, the café has booster seats but no high chairs. A better bet for a quick bite might be one of the many inexpensive places around Dupont Circle. For pizza, gyros, and other Greek concoctions made with tomato and cheese, try **Zorba's Café** (1612 20th St. NW, tel. 202/387–8555). At **Kramer Books and Afterwards Café** (1517 Connecticut Ave. NW, tel. 202/387–3825), enjoy a book with breakfast, lunch, or dinner.

1600 21st St. NW.
Metro: Dupont Circle

 202/387-2151;
www.phillipscollection.org

 Weekday admission free with
suggested donation, weekends
$12 adults, children 18 and
under free. Fees for special
exhibits vary

 T–Sa 10–5, Su 11–6 (Su summer hrs
may vary), open Th until 8:30 PM

 5 and up, workshops
6 and up

Paul Klee also appeal to kids. His small-scale paintings include many kinds of symbols—even some that look like hieroglyphic symbols. But perhaps the artwork that will have the greatest impact is on the bottom floor of the museum's Sant building where works by local students through the Young Artists Exhibition Program are on display.

Gather a group of five or more kids (and call four weeks in advance) for a personal tour. The tour includes interactive activities led by the museum's enthusiastic education staff. If you don't have time to book an advance tour or if the idea of being with more than a couple of kids seems daunting, you can call ahead for a family fun pack (and impress your kids with your knowledge) or pick one up at the museum's entrance or download activity sheets from the Web site. Each pack includes artwork to discover, postcards or pictures, and activities you can try at home so the fun continues long after you've left.

If you like this sight you may also like the National Gallery of Art (#33).

MAKE THE MOST OF YOUR TIME

During the gallery's popular Family Free Days, held annually the first weekend in June, you can take part in projects (on a walk-in basis) that could entail anything from creative crafts, special tours, and live music. Throughout the year, hands-on workshops for children and their parents ($15–$20 per adult-child pair) revolve around special exhibits and themes. Kids might find themselves at a photo shoot or making a sculpture.

ROCK CREEK PARK

On the biggest stretch of parkland in Washington you can truly take a walk on the wild side. Begin at the nature center, which brings the outdoors in. Pelts, bones, feathers, and a bird's nest occupy a touch table in the lobby, while another room contains stuffed animals representative of the park. Preschoolers put on puppet shows featuring their forest friends in the Discovery Room. Downstairs, elementary schoolchildren use mice (the computer kind) to discover even more about the park's ecosystem. A 75-seat planetarium introduces youngsters to the solar system, and some shows include a Native American legend about a coyote that threw rocks to make pictures in the sky.

Take a hike on any of several trails near the center, but first pick up a discovery pack for each child at the front desk. Packs are equipped with binoculars, a magnifying lens, and a chart for recording the birds you see. The 15- to 20-minute Edge of the Woods trail, a flat, asphalt loop perfect for preschoolers and strollers, goes to a pond a little larger than a bathtub, where tadpoles swim in spring. For older children, the Woodland Trail takes 40–

EATS FOR KIDS To wet your whistle, you can get a sip from the water fountain or purchase a bottle of water at the center. For anything else, you're on your own, but picnic areas are near the nature center. Pack a lunch from **Magruder's Grocery Store** (3627 Connecticut Ave. NW, tel. 202/237–2531), a 5- to 10-minute drive from the nature center. Near Magruder's are two inexpensive restaurants: **American City Diner** (5532 Connecticut Ave. NW, tel. 202/244–1949) and **Bread and Chocolate** (5542 Connecticut Ave. NW, tel. 202/966–7413), for those who want a more healthful meal with an elegant dessert. If your child doesn't care for éclairs or other pastries, don't worry; cookies are available, too.

5200 Glover Rd. NW; stables
5100 Glover Rd. NW (between 16th St. and
Connecticut Ave., south of Military Rd.)

Free; pony rides
$20 for 15 min;
trail rides
$30 per hr

Daily sunrise–sunset; nature center
W–Su 9–5; pony rides Apr–Oct T, W, Th
3 and 3:30, Sa–Su 1–3:30, trail rides
T, W and Th 6, Su 11–12:30

2 and up, pony rides 4–7,
trail rides 12 and up

202/895-6070 nature center,
202/362-0117 stables; www.nps.gov/rocr/

60 minutes, depending on how often you stop to search for animals crawling on the forest floor or chirping atop the trees. On most weekends, rangers lead hikes on topics ranging from the lowly worm to the majestic wolf.

Take to the saddle: Rock Creek is the only place in town where kids can become urban cowboys and cowgirls (closed-toe shoes, preferably with a small heel, are required). Pony rides (reservations required) aren't just a trip around a circle; they're 15-minute rides in the woods. They'll take children as young as 2½ and as old as 11, but many preschoolers aren't ready for this excursion, and kids over 8 might find it babyish, since a teenage guide holds the reins. Before and after, kids are encouraged to pat their pony. On 1-hour trail rides, guides take groups along some of the same wooded trails that presidents Martin Van Buren, Teddy Roosevelt, and Ronald Reagan and World War II general George Patton once rode.

MAKE THE MOST OF YOUR TIME

The planetarium offers free weekend shows for different age ranges. Children 4 and under may find the shows either boring or scary. At the end of the show, the rangers will give you a sheet showing the stars that you can see in the sky that month.

KEEP IN MIND If your child is 6–12, ask for a Junior Ranger activity book. When your child completes at least five of the eight activities, show the book to a ranger, so your youngster's hard work can be rewarded with a signed certificate and a Junior Ranger patch with a picture of a boulder bridge that goes over the Creek.

ROOSEVELT ISLAND

If the wildest animal your children ever want to see is a computer mouse, Roosevelt Island isn't for your family. But for kids who believe, as Theodore Roosevelt did, that "There is delight in the hardy life of the open," this sanctuary is a superb place to get away from the city's concrete, crowds, and cars. If it weren't for the airplanes from Ronald Reagan National Airport roaring overhead, you might forget you were in D.C. altogether.

Leave your car in the parking lot next to the George Washington Memorial Parkway and walk over the bridge to this island wilderness preserve in the Potomac River. The 88.5-acre tribute to the conservation-minded 26th president includes 2½ mi of nature trails that crisscross marshland, swampland, and upland forest.

In the center of the island is a clearing, where a 17-foot bronze statue of Roosevelt stands, his right hand raised for emphasis. He is surrounded by shallow pools, fountains, and four large stone tablets inscribed with his thoughts on nature, manhood, state

KEEP IN MIND How did the Rough Rider known for carrying "a big stick" inspire a stuffed animal? Once, when Roosevelt was hunting, his aides tied up an old bear for him to kill. But he couldn't shoot the defenseless animal, prompting a toy maker to create the teddy bear.

MAKE THE MOST OF YOUR TIME After you cross the bridge, you can see a large bulletin board where you can pick up a brochure with a map. Encourage your children to stay on the marked trails. Off the trails you may encounter poison ivy and great nettles, some as tall as 3 feet, better known as stinging nettles because you can feel a stinging pain if you rub against it. Gather a group of 10 or more people and call two weeks in advance to request a guided tour led by a park ranger, who will point out a lot more than where the stinging nettles are.

(government), and youth. For example, he advised students at the Groton School in Massachusetts, "Keep your eyes on the stars, but remember to keep your feet on the ground." And there is plenty of ground for your feet to cover at Roosevelt Island.

To make the most of your visit, pack a backpack with some of the following items for your children: binoculars, a magnifying glass, a sketch pad and crayons or markers, a camera, and plant and animal guidebooks, if you have them. Cattails, arrow arum, pickerelweed, willow, ash, maple, and oak all grow on the island, which is also a habitat for frogs, raccoons, birds, squirrels, deer, and the occasional red or gray fox. But you won't see the animal most people associate with Roosevelt: the teddy bear.

If you like this sight, you may also like Discovery Creek Children's Museum (#56).

EATS FOR KIDS There's nothing to buy on this island—not even a soda. You may not want to drink too much anyway, since public restrooms close between late October and early April. If you're coming from D.C., consider a stop in Georgetown first. You can pick up sandwiches, fried chicken, and salads at **Safeway** (1855 Wisconsin Ave. NW, tel. 202/333-3223). The Park Service requests that you don't eat too close to the memorial, and there aren't any picnic tables so you'll want to bring a blanket. Listen to the music of birds and the planes overhead as you eat.

SACKLER GALLERY/FREER
GALLERY OF ART

Imagine your children making an animal paperweight or sketching on a scroll while learning about ancient art techniques, geography, or other cultures. It's all part of the ImaginAsia program. Armed with guidebook and pencil, children (and their parents) search for ceramics, sculpture, and paintings and then go beyond simply writing about what they see. They may locate on a map where a work or an artist is from, interpret works, describe how they feel, or even invent stories. Afterward, you all meet in an education room, where your kids can create a take-home craft related to the exhibits seen. The program is operated on a drop-in basis; reservations are only required for groups of eight or more.

Even if you're not visiting on a program day, there's plenty here to interest your kids. Activity-filled guidebooks are available at each museum's information desk. And just why are there two Asian museums, you might be wondering? The Freer Gallery, which contains one of the world's finest collections of Asian masterpieces, was endowed by Charles Freer, who insisted on a few conditions: Objects in the collection could not be loaned out, nor could objects from outside the collection be put on display. Because of the latter, the connected Sackler

MAKE THE MOST OF YOUR TIME The "education" section of the galleries' Web site provides a useful guide for teachers that can also inform which collections would be most appropriate and interesting for your family.

Freer: 12th St. and Jefferson Dr. SW, Sackler: 1050 Independence Ave. SW; Metro: Smithsonian

 Free

 Daily 10–5:30

202/633-1000, 202/357-1729 TTY; www.asia.si.edu

2 and up, ImaginAsia 6–14

Gallery was built. Like the Freer, the Sackler focuses on works from throughout Asia, but it also mounts visiting exhibits. The Freer's exhibits do change to rotate its massive collection.

The Freer's collection also includes works by American artists influenced by Asia. One such was Freer's friend James McNeill Whistler, who introduced him to Asian art. On display in Gallery 12 is Whistler's Peacock Room, a blue-and-gold painted dining room, decorated with painted leather, wood, and canvas and, as the name implies, devoted to peacocks. Freer paid $42,000 for the entire room and moved it from London to the United States in 1904. Perhaps your children will be influenced by the Asian masterpieces they see or inspired to decorate their bedrooms with a particular theme (you might have to increase their allowance!).

If you like this sight you may also like National Museum of African Art (#31).

EATS FOR KIDS
For restaurant choices, see any of the listings for museums on the Mall: the Castle, Museum of the American Indian, National Air and Space Museum, National Gallery of Art and Sculpture Garden, National Museum of American History, and National Museum of Natural History.

KEEP IN MIND While you're in the Peacock Room, think about the real peacocks that used to live at the gallery. In 1993 a peacock named James and a peahen named Sylvia resided in the museum's courtyard. After one year, the gallery needed to find a new home for the birds because Sylvia laid too many eggs. James and Sylvia lived with a farmer who loved them because they squawked to alert her when visitors arrived.

SIX FLAGS AMERICA

Washington is known for attractions that are educational and economical; Six Flags America is neither, but it's exciting. Actually a combination theme park and water park (dubbed Hurricane Harbor), it contains more than 100 rides, shows, and games spread over 150 acres.

On the "dry" side, roller-coaster revelers have eight fast choices. The Wild One is a more-than-85-year-old classic wooden coaster. Roar mixes old-fashioned wood and modern computer technology to produce a thrilling ride. The five steel coasters are Batwing, Superman-Ride of Steel, the Mind Eraser, the Joker's Jinx, and Two-Face: The Flip Side, which takes you through a 72-foot-high vertical loop—twice. Coaster traditionalists prefer the jiggle and clackety-clack sounds of the "woodie." Metal coasters follow a more circuitous route, with corkscrew turns and 360-degree loops. If your youngsters aren't tall enough (all rides, including the coasters, have height restrictions), head to Looney Tunes Movie Town, where

MAKE THE MOST OF YOUR TIME Lines form on weekends before the park opens. To avoid crowds, go on Monday or Tuesday. If you're spending time at Hurricane Harbor Water Park, plan on getting out of your wet swimsuits a bit early. The "wet side" closes one hour before the park does.

EATS FOR KIDS Approximately 10,000 pounds of sugar are used to make the roughly 100,000 servings of candy sold here each year—the same amount you'd use if you felt like baking nearly 1½ million chocolate-chip cookies. That said, no outside food is permitted, though you can bring in one sealed bottle of water per person. Vendors provide complimentary cups of water and ice. The **Hollywood Backlot Café, Heritage House,** and **Crazy Horse Saloon** are air-conditioned.

13710 Central Ave.
(Rte. 214), Largo, MD

 301/249–1500;
www.sixflags.com

 $49.99 over 54", $28.99
children 4 and up or 54"
and under (add 10% en-
tertainment tax); parking
$15, 3 and under free

 M–F 10:30–6, Sa–Su 10:30–9; Mid-Apr–May,
Sa–Su 10:30–6; hours vary during summer

 2 and up

even toddlers can coast on a minicoaster, get behind the wheel of pint-size 18-wheeler, or earn their wings by flying minijets.

On the "wet" side, kids like Crocodile Cal's Caribbean Beach House. Water-powered activities here include a barrel that dumps 1,000 gallons of water on unsuspecting passersby every few minutes. The Hurricane Bay wave pool has a graduated entrance so even water babies (with parents, of course) can splash around, but an even better bet for little ones might be Buccaneer Beach. In a twist of the height restrictions, anyone over 54" must be accompanied by a child.

If you like this sight, you may also like Medieval Times Dinner & Tournament (#42).

KEEP IN MIND To minimize expenses and aggravation, prepare ahead. Look for discount coupons at grocery stores, or consider a season pass, which includes discounts at other Six Flags parks. If your child (or your arms) needs a stroller, bring your own to save the rental fee; most families end up spending about six to eight hours here.

SMITHSONIAN AMERICAN ART
MUSEUM AND THE NATIONAL PORTRAIT GALLERY

You've got a two-for-one visit here. Both the Museum of American Art and the National Portrait Gallery share space in this building built in the mid-1800s. Both museums were recently renovated. Both museums are part of the Smithsonian Institution. But the museums are different.

The work in the Smithsonian American Art Museum, emphasizes art, rather than the subject. This museum is the home of one of the largest collections of American art in the world, including craft and folk art that kids can relate to. More than 41,000 artworks span more than three centuries.

At the National Portrait Gallery, the emphasis is on the subject. It's like a "Who's Who?" of Americans who have shaped our country. From presidents to sports heroes to military figures, they're here in some form, including photographs, paintings, sculptures, and drawings.

MAKE THE MOST OF YOUR TIME The two museums share the Lunder Conservation Center on the third floor, where you can see the techniques used to examine, treat, and preserve artwork. If a conservator isn't at work when you arrive, you can watch a 40-foot media wall that shows them at work. Of course, before art can be preserved, it must be created. Don't be surprised if your kids go a little crazy with aluminum foil when you get home!

8th and F Sts. NW

 Free

Daily 11:30–5:30

202/633-1000; americanart.si.edu
or www.npg.si.edu

4 and up

To the left of the shared main lobby is the art museum. Ask your son what he would do with an empty garage. Ask your daughter what she would do with hundreds of rolls of aluminum foil. Check out what James Hampton did when he was working as a janitor. For more than 12 years he built a huge throne using salvaged objects and what amounts to reams of silver and gold foils. His shiny *Throne of the Third Heaven of the Nations Millennium General Assembly,* referred to as the Throne, captivates kids of all ages. An unknown artist created *Bottlecap Giraffe* in the late 1960s. (No word on whether he or she drank all the sodas to get the caps.) Another artist, Nam June Paik, created a piece called *Electronic Superhighway: Continental U.S., Alaska, Hawaii,* using 343 televisions.

If you like this sight you may also like the sculpture gardens at the National Gallery of Art (#33).

EATS FOR KIDS

A **café** in a courtyard serves American fare. You can also try the **food court** in the Technology Center (800 K St., no phone).

KEEP IN MIND Most large museums have many more objects in storage than what's on display. The American Art museum is different. Even if your child isn't impressed that the Luce Foundation Center's cabinets and glass cases hold 3,500 objects, he or she might have fun opening the drawers to see miniatures and medals. You can pick up a scavenger hunt sheet for the Luce Foundation Center at the Center's information desk on the mezzanine.

SULLY HISTORIC SITE

As at other local historic sites, kids can get a real feel for how people lived two centuries ago at this museum dedicated to life in the Federal Period (1790–1820). Your children may pretend to wash dishes in an old stone sink, cool off with a folded fan, or use sugar nippers. They may soak up the scent of the green and black teas that were popular at the time or get a whiff of No. 7, a cologne that George Washington (and more recently John F. Kennedy) wore. But kids also learn that life wasn't so sweet then, and not just because the early 1800s lacked our modern amenities. Slavery, too, is addressed, and your children can handle replicas of the passes that slaves needed to leave the property or lift the heavy cast ironware used in the kitchen.

Sully was the understated 1794 country home of Richard Bland Lee, uncle of Confederate general Robert E. Lee; his wife, Elizabeth Collins Lee; and their children. As Virginia's first representative to Congress, Lee cast one of two swing votes that put the nation's capital in his backyard.

KEEP IN MIND Some of the stairs in the Sully mansion are steep, so make sure unsteady toddlers, unsteady grandparents, and distracted parents are extra careful. Strollers are not permitted in the house, but the first floor is wheelchair accessible.

MAKE THE MOST OF YOUR TIME At least one weekend each month, Sully hosts special events. For example, Father's Day is the car show, the Sunday after Labor Day is the quilt show, and the first Saturday in November Sully celebrates Colonial Day. Admission is a dollar or two more during special events but there's more to do and see.

3601 Sully Rd., Chantilly, VA

 703/437–1794;
www.fairfaxcounty.gov/parks/sully

 $6 adults, $5 students 16
and up, $4 children 5–15

 W–M 11–4

5 and up

Purchase tickets and even souvenirs in a one-room, log schoolhouse that was used in nearby Haymarket during the early to mid-19th century. In this tiny room, about a half-dozen children studied under a teacher who lived above the classroom.

Guides, often Fairfax County Park Authority volunteers, conduct one-hour tours of the Lee house on the hour. If the guides don't point it out, challenge your child to find the white squirrel in the parlor. When the Lee children were living here, their pet white squirrel was let loose in the house! Upon request, the guides may tailor their talk to your family's special interests (textiles or cooking, for example). Weather permitting, there is also the Forgotten Road Tour of the outbuildings, including reconstructed slave dwellings, at 2 (early March–mid-November). Most spring and summer weekends are especially festive, with such special events as quill pen writing, biscuit baking, and children's games.

If you like this sight you may also like the Children's Museum of Rose Hill Manor Park (#62).

EATS FOR KIDS In the little **schoolhouse** you can purchase candy sticks, a treat that kids have enjoyed since the 1800s, and other candies. Or head to **Milwaukee Custard** (13934 Lee Jackson Memorial Hwy., tel. 703/263–1920) for creamy custard year-round and Italian ices in summer. Inside, trains whiz overhead and photos of kids with custard on their faces adorn the walls. Call a week in advance to arrange a tour of the shop that ends with a free sample. Or visit friendly **Golden China** (13934 Metrotech Dr., tel. 703/ 631–8889) for food that 21st-century kids enjoy.

THOMAS JEFFERSON MEMORIAL

Many children and adults may be surprised to learn that Thomas Jefferson didn't list being president as one of his greatest accomplishments. When he appraised his own life, Jefferson wanted to be remembered as the "Author of the Declaration of American Independence, of the Statute of Virginia for religious freedom, and Father of the University of Virginia."

The memorial honoring the third president is the southernmost of the District's major monuments and memorials, four long blocks and a trip around the Tidal Basin from the Metro. Jefferson had always admired the Pantheon in Rome (the rotundas he designed for the University of Virginia and his own Monticello were inspired by its dome), so architect John Russell Pope drew from the same source when he designed this memorial. But even children who have never heard of Rome, not to mention Jefferson, can still enjoy one of the city's best views of the White House from the memorial's top steps.

KEEP IN MIND Every spring, Washington eagerly waits for the delicate flowers of the cherry trees to bloom (many of which are near the memorial). Park-service experts try their best to predict when the buds will pop—usually for about 10–12 days at the beginning of April. But regardless of when they flower, the two-week long National Cherry Blossom Festival (tel. 202/547–1500 for dates and information) is celebrated with the lighting of a ceremonial Japanese lantern, fashion shows, and a parade. When the weather complies and the blossoms are at their peak for the festival, Washington rejoices.

Tidal Basin South Bank. Metro: Smithsonian

 24 hrs; staffed daily 9:30 AM–8 PM

 Free

202/426–6841; www.nps.gov/thje

5 and up

Inside the memorial a 19-foot bronze statue of Jefferson on a 6-foot granite pedestal looms larger than life. And just in case your children didn't take the National Park Service ranger recommendation to research Jefferson before visiting the memorial, they can learn about this Renaissance man by reading his writings about freedom and government on marble walls surrounding the statue. The whole family can take advantage of ranger programs offered throughout the day or ask questions of the ranger on duty.

An exhibit called Light and Liberty, on the lower level, provides highlights of Jefferson's life, a timeline of world history during his lifetime and a 10-minute video. When you've seen it all, you and your children can judge for yourselves what Jefferson's greatest accomplishments really were.

If you like this sight you may also like the Lincoln Memorial (#44).

EATS FOR KIDS
Rumor has it that some critics called the memorial "Jefferson's muffin" based on its shape. A short drive away in East Potomac Park is **Potomac Grill** (110 Ohio Dr. SW, at Maine Ave., tel. 202/554–7660) where you can get bran, corn, and banana muffins in addition to jumbo burgers and sandwiches at more reasonable prices than most Mall vendors. There's also a minigolf course there.

MAKE THE MOST OF YOUR TIME Allow about five hours to tour the monuments in Washington. From mid-April through November, you might want to set aside an hour for a paddleboat ride in the Tidal Basin (1501 Maine Ave. SW, tel. 202/479–2426; www.tidalbasinpeddleboats.com). You can see the dock from the Memorial.

UNITED STATES BOTANIC GARDEN

Follow your nose. Or your eyes. Or your sense of humor. Or just follow the meandering paths around the amazing conservatory here. It's full of gardens to delight the senses and tickle the fancy with exotic, strange, rare, and beautiful plants from all over the world.

George Washington, Thomas Jefferson, and James Madison imagined a national botanic garden. Congress established the garden in 1820, the first greenhouse opened in 1842, and the conservatory was completed in 1933. This national treasure, the delight of botany lovers big and small, is more magnificent than the Founding Fathers could have imagined.

Kids can see plants that dinosaurs might have munched on in the Garden Primeval. Look down at the pathway for footprints from baby and grown-up dinosaurs. To learn how plants grow to become today's products, from fragrances to food, head to the Garden Court. See how bananas grow upside down from 20-foot stalks. Then check out the therapeutic uses of the specimens in Medicinal Plants.

KEEP IN MIND Read the signs carefully. With the exception of the Children's Garden kids should not touch plants unless the staff invites them to feel a particular one. Allow at least an hour to see what's in bloom when you visit and to plant some seeds of wisdom in your own little gardeners.

MAKE THE MOST OF YOUR TIME If you'd like to chase a few butterflies or just need to get your child outside, take time to explore the National Gardens that opened in October 2006. The butterfly garden is just one attraction of this garden with native plants and a First Ladies Water Garden with a mosaic water fountain that you can dip your toes in. You can also enter the gardens from Independence Avenue or Maryland Avenue.

100 Maryland Ave. SW.
Metro: Federal Center Southwest

Free

Daily 10–5

202/225-8333; www.usbg.gov

2 and up

In World Deserts, cacti grow sharp spines (some of which look like fishhooks) as protection from grazing animals, though of course they aren't in any danger here. A sign explains how cacti expand and contract like accordions. Children may not be as enchanted about orchids until they discover more about this diverse flowering family. For example, the beard orchid looks like it sprouted whiskers, and the mirror orchid attracts male wasps because its flowers look like female wasps.

To really dig in, head to the Children's Garden (open spring–summer) where children can try out gardening tools, meander through a tunnel made of bamboo and hang out in a thatched roof cottage the size of a playhouse. Push the hand pump and watch a fish spout water into a fountain.

If you like this sight you may also like the U.S. National Arboretum (#9).

EATS FOR KIDS Though orchids hardly look appetizing, some kinds of vanilla ice cream contain flavoring from the cured seedpod of an orchid called *Vanilla planifolia*. For ice cream and other foods, check out the eateries under the United States Capitol, the National Museum of the American Indian, the National Gallery of Art, and the National Air and Space Museum. On a pleasant day, bring your meal over to Bartholdi Park, across Independence Avenue from the Conservatory. Frédéric Auguste Bartholdi, designer of the huge historic fountain, is best known for designing the Statue of Liberty.

UNITED STATES CAPITOL

Throughout the Capitol, statues, paintings, and even rooms reveal much about the people and events that shaped our nation. The frieze around the rim of the Rotunda depicts 400 years of recognizable American history. Columbus's arrival, the California Gold Rush, and the Wright brothers' historic flight are all here. Eight immense oil paintings depict historical scenes, four from the Revolutionary War period. See if your child can find Pocahontas in the Rotunda. (*Hint*: She's in three places, and she doesn't resemble Disney's cartoon.)

You have two ways to see this symbol of democratic government. You can wait in line for a timed entry ticket for that day, which will yield a tour guided by the United Capitol Guide Service (accustomed to taking school groups around). In winter, the wait might only be five minutes for tickets; in spring and summer, people are in line by 7 AM. Everyone must be present to receive tickets.

MAKE THE MOST OF YOUR TIME To take the 30-minute guided tour, plan for at least another 30 minutes of waiting and going through security. To enhance your children's experience, talk about Congress's role in our government and the Capitol's place in history before you arrive. Then during the tour, encourage them to move up front to see and hear better. Sometimes kids want to know how long it took to build the Capitol. The answer: 200 years and still building.

East end of Mall. Metro: Capitol South, Federal Triangle

 202/224–3121, 202/225–6827 recording, 202/224–4049 TDD; www.aoc.gov

 Free, timed-entry passes given out beginning at 9 AM at the kiosk at 1st St. and Independence Ave. SW until the visitor center opens (expected completion 2008).

 M–Sa 9–4; hrs subject to change

7 and up

Another route for getting a tour is contacting your congressperson's office and ask what services they provide. A staffer might provide a personalized tour or they may get you tickets for tours with the guide service, saving you from getting in line.

Free gallery passes to watch the House or Senate in session can be obtained only from your senator's or representative's office either in advance or when you're already in the Capitol.

Even if you don't see your representative or senator, you'll find statues of people representing each state in National Statuary Hall. Ask your guide for help finding your states' statues. They range from Colorado's (and *Apollo 13*'s) Jack Swigert to Utah's Philo Farnsworth, the father of TV. With a solid granite base of six tons, Hawaii's Kamehameha I in Statuary Hall is one of the heaviest in the collection.

If you like this sight, you may also like the White House (#2).

KEEP IN MIND
In National Statuary Hall, strange things happen to sound. A slight whisper spoken on one side of the hall can be heard on the other. If the room isn't too noisy during your tour, the trick may work.

EATS FOR KIDS When the visitor center opens, it will have a 550-seat cafeteria. Until then, you can dine in the **North Servery**, open from 7:30 to 3 PM, except when the Senate is in session when it closes from noon to 1:30, or the **South Buffet** in the basement of the Dirksen Building (202/224–7196). Adventurous eaters might want to try the Senate bean soup, a favorite with legislators since 1901. The **Longworth Food Court** (tel. 202/225–0878; open 7:30–2:30), on the House side, offers Chinese, Greek, Italian, barbecue, and deli food.

UNITED STATES HOLOCAUST
MEMORIAL MUSEUM

Like the history it covers, the Holocaust Museum can be profoundly moving and emotionally complex, so you should first decide whether your children can appreciate it. The recommended ages published by the museum are guidelines only. During the busy tourist season (March–August), the museum is often crowded, making it difficult to obtain tickets (details below). The average visit is long, often 2–3 hours, and exhibits involve lots of reading. All that said, a trip here will be memorable for a preteen or teenager.

You don't need a pass for Remember the Children: Daniel's Story, an exhibit that tells the history of the Holocaust through the perspective of a young boy growing up in Nazi Germany. Children know from the beginning that Daniel survives to share his story. In this interactive exhibit, your children can follow events in Daniel's life. For example, they can see and touch his family's suitcases and clothing, and look into their ghetto apartment. At the end of the exhibit, kids are invited to write about their thoughts and feelings. It's a helpful outlet after this moving experience.

EATS FOR KIDS The museum's **café,** open 8:30–4:30, offers a variety of dishes, including matzoh-ball soup and potato knishes, kosher Asian-noodle salads, and even peanut butter and jelly sandwiches.

MAKE THE MOST OF YOUR TIME You will need a same-day, timed-entry pass to get into the permanent exhibition, which you can obtain at the museum on the day of your visit. For advance tickets, go through tickets.com (tel. 800/400–9373, 888/331–6774 TTY). Ideally, it might be best for you to visit the museum without your children first to determine its appropriateness for your family. If that's not possible, consider going through Daniel's Story first.

The museum's main exhibition tells the story of the 11 million Jews, Gypsies, Poles, Jehovah's Witnesses, homosexuals, political prisoners, and others killed by the Nazis between 1933 and 1945. Striving to give a realistic first-person experience, the graphic presentation is as extraordinary as the subject matter: upon arrival, each visitor is issued an "identity card" containing biographical information on a real person from the Holocaust. As you move through the museum, you read sequential updates on your card. The museum recounts the Holocaust through documentary films, videotaped and audiotaped oral histories, and a collection that includes such items as a freight car, like those used to transport Jews from Warsaw to the Treblinka death camp. Although there are four privacy walls to protect visitors from especially graphic images, they don't cover all that is horrific. After this powerful experience, the adjacent Hall of Remembrance provides space for quiet reflection.

If you like this sight you may also like the Vietnam Veterans Memorial (#7).

KEEP IN MIND Kids have shown they care and they will remember. More than 3,000 American schoolchildren painted their feelings on porcelain for the Children's Children's Tile Wall on the lower level. They painted flowers, peace signs, clasped hands, many versions of the word "hope," and more in this moving tribute.

UNITED STATES NATIONAL ARBORETUM

How does your garden grow? Here the garden grows with priceless, 350-year-old trees smaller than a 2-year-old, herbs, an aquatic garden, and 15,000 magnificent azaleas. The arboretum has two entrances: New York Avenue and R Street, off Bladensburg Road. Whichever you choose, your first stop should be the administration building, where you can see speckled, bright orange koi flourishing in the surrounding pool. Some are as long as a child's arm, others as little as a finger. You can watch the staff feed the fish on Tuesday and Thursday at 10:30 from May to October. Pick up a map inside. You'll need it. Almost 10 mi of winding roads cover 446 acres of botanical masterpieces.

Make sure you visit the National Bonsai & Penjing Museum. (In Japan artistic potted plants are bonsai and in China tray landscapes are called *penjing*.) These arts have been depicted in Chinese paintings as early as the sixth century. The idea is simple: just as you get your hair cut to achieve a desired look, so these trees are trimmed for a desired look, which varies by species. The trees are worth "about as much as your children," according to the curator.

MAKE THE MOST OF YOUR TIME You may drive, bike, walk, or do a little of each around the arboretum. Walking is pleasant, especially with a stroller, but you can't cover much ground. You can bike, and there are even racks for locking your bicycle scattered around. Driving is slow—the speed limit is 20 mph and enforced—but you can park at each garden/museum within the arboretum. There's a tram that runs on weekends and holidays, mid-April through mid-October ($4 adults, $2 children 4–16). The 40-minute ride may be good for older kids who are really into horticulture, but it doesn't make stops, so it's not ideal for an intensive look at the gardens.

3501 New York Ave. NE

 Free

 Daily 8–5; National Bonsai &
Penjing Museum daily 10–3:30

 202/245-2726;
www.usna.usda.gov

2 and up

Many have been nurtured for generations, and some were gifts to presidents. Your children might enjoy wandering through outdoor rooms in search of the oldest trees, the smallest trees, or those with interesting trunks. Follow your nose to the National Herb Garden, where herbs from around the world are arranged. Kids can have fun sniffing out aloe, oregano, wild strawberries, licorice, English lavender, and ginger. Hundreds of heritage roses also bloom here. Fruits, vegetables, and flowers thrive in the Youth Garden, planted by schoolkids, who share what they grow with the homeless.

But plants aren't the only things jutting out from the earth. Twenty-two sandstone Corinthian columns that once stood at the east portico of the U.S. Capitol are set in a rectangle on a hill in a meadow.

If you like this sight, you may also like the Kenilworth National Aquatic Gardens (#46).

KEEP IN MIND Do you know your state tree? At the National Grove of State Trees, you can search for the official trees of all 50 states and the District of Columbia. Pick up a state tree list at the administration building. Don't look for markers on the ground; identification tags hang from the branches.

EATS FOR KIDS (For a quarter, you can buy food for the fish and watch them swallow their pellets whole. Look for machines that look like they would contain gumballs. But beware that the pellet dispensers are filled on Saturday mornings in summer so they're often empty by Saturday afternoon.) When you're ready to feed your children, don't be tempted to pick the fruits, vegetables, or herbs, no matter how delicious they appear. (Think the Garden of Eden.) A vendor serving coffee, smoothies, and muffins comes sporadically throughout summer weekends. Your best bet is to pack your own food and dine on the terrace.

U.S. NAVY MUSEUM

This museum is a sure bet for any child interested in things military. Just call 24 hours ahead for a reservation and your kids can spin the wheels of sailing ships, peer through periscopes, and turn and elevate 40-milimeter long guns from World War II. All the while, they can get a maritime perspective on American history from the American Revolution to the present, including learning about the Navy's peacetime pursuits, such as diplomacy and humanitarian service. The U.S. Navy Museum is an especially good place to visit with a friend or relative who has served in the military.

Hands-on activities range from the no-tech, such as knot tying, to the high-tech, such as a Battle of Midway computer game in which children decipher coded messages. Free brochures listing activities for kids of all ages are available at the front desk. A kindergartner might do something as simple as draw a hat on a sailor or connect dots to make a plane; older kids are encouraged to search for a silver sailor created from dimes or write slogans encouraging military service.

MAKE THE MOST OF YOUR TIME The nearest Metro stop, Eastern Market, is 15–20 minutes away, and though the Navy Yard is secure, the surrounding neighborhood isn't always safe in the evening. So especially if you're planning to stay until closing, it's best to drive. Call for directions. Parking is free and plentiful.

Washington Navy Yard, 9th and M Sts. SE

 M–F 9–5; weekends and holidays 10–5 (Call by noon on Friday for weekend visitation); USS *Barry* M–F 9–5, weekends and holidays 10–5

 Free

202/433–4882;
www.history.navy.mil

5 and up

If you call a few weeks in advance, you can arrange a special tour for your family or group. Themes include Hats Off, during which kids learn about naval occupations by studying hats and then creating their own, and To the Ends of the Earth and Beyond, in which middle-schoolers study the Navy's role in polar and underwater explorations.

Outside the museum your family can board the decommissioned *Barry,* a destroyer used during the Cuban Missile Crisis and the Vietnam War. Kids like the narrow halls, bunk beds, and mess hall, but they love taking the captain's wheel to "steer" the ship. Ahoy mates!

If you like this sight you may also like the U.S. Navy Memorial across from the National Archives (#36).

KEEP IN MIND
If your children say they want to become sailors, tell them about the "powder monkeys." During the War of 1812, Mexican War, and Civil War, sailors—always boys, as young as 9—carried gun-powder from the magazine to the guns. It was a dangerous job, because these lads were often the targets of enemy fire.

EATS FOR KIDS During the week, dine in or carry out food from the Navy Yard's **food court** and familiar harbors **Subway, Dunkin' Donuts,** and **McDonald's.** On weekends, you have to bring your own meals. You can picnic any day of the week alongside seagulls at waterside picnic tables in the shade or sun.

VIETNAM VETERANS MEMORIAL

Sometimes kids ask some serious questions about war and death after visiting this moving memorial to the 58,253 men and women who died in Vietnam. Sometimes children think they're all buried at the monument. They aren't, of course, but the slabs of black granite inscribed with the names of the dead are as somber, as powerful, and as evocative of poignant reflection as any cemetery.

Known as "the Wall," the memorial is one of the most visited sites in Washington. Conceived by Jan Scruggs, a former infantry corporal who had served in Vietnam, these black granite panels that reflect the sky, the trees, and the faces of those looking for names (and perhaps crying when they find them) were designed by Maya Ying Lin, a 21-year-old architectural student at Yale. The nontraditional war memorial was originally decried by some veterans, but with the addition of a flagpole just south of the Wall as well as Frederick Hart's statue of three soldiers, most critics were won over.

EATS FOR KIDS Grab a hot dog or hamburger at a **food kiosk** behind the nearby Korean War Veterans Memorial.

MAKE THE MOST OF YOUR TIME Decode the symbols. Every name is preceded (on the West Wall) or followed (on the East Wall) by a symbol designating status. A diamond indicates "killed, body recovered." A small percentage of names have plus signs, indicating "killed: body not recovered." Several hundred remains of men have been found and identified, so the symbols next to their names were changed to diamonds. If a man returns alive, a circle, as a symbol of life, will be inscribed around the plus sign. Alas, there have not been any circles added.

Constitution Gardens, 22nd St. and
Constitution Ave. NW. Metro: Foggy Bottom

 Free

  24 hrs; staffed daily 8 AM–midnight

 202/634–4568; www.nps.gov/vive

9 and up

People's names appear on the Wall in the order of the date they died. To look up a name yourself, refer to the books posted at the entrance and exit of the memorial or ask at the white kiosk with the brown roof near the entrance. At the wall, rangers and volunteers wearing yellow caps can look up names and supply you with graphite pencils and paper to make rubbings of names.

Thousands of offerings are left at the wall each year. While many people still leave flowers, remembrances have been evolving, from personal objects such as letters from soldiers and clothing they wore to thank-you letters from schoolchildren.

If you like this sight you may also like the World War II Memorial and the Korean War Memorial nearby. How does each memorial pay tribute to the soldiers who served? Encourage your child to talk with the park rangers at each site.

KEEP IN MIND Many people are surprised to learn that although 10,000 women served in Vietnam, only eight women's names are on the Wall. One of these is Mary Klinker, a nurse involved in Operation Baby Lift, a mission to bring Vietnamese orphans to the United States. Klinker's plane crashed in 1975.

WASHINGTON MONUMENT

Some kids say the Washington Monument looks like a giant pencil. Others think this 555'5.9" obelisk (10 times as tall as its width at the base) punctuates the capital like a huge, partially buried exclamation point. Visible from nearly everywhere in the city, it's a landmark for visiting tourists and lost motorists alike and a beacon for anyone who yearns to shoot to the top and survey all of Washington below.

A limited number of free tickets, good for a half-hour period, are available beginning at 8 AM at the marble lodge on 15th Street that was reopened after restoration in 2007. Advance tickets are available from recreation.gov. Arrive at the monument at the appointed time. Although lines to get in may be long, they move quickly. If your children are restless, have them count the flags surrounding the monument. (There are 50: one for each state, though none for the District of Columbia.) Once you're inside, an elevator whizzes to the top in just 70 seconds, a trip that originally took about 12 minutes in a steam-powered elevator back in 1888 when the monument opened to visitors.

KEEP IN MIND A lot of people are curious about the color change about a third of the way up on the monument. It took more than 50 years to build this monument. Fundraising began in 1833, and the cornerstone was laid in 1848. However, by 1854, construction had stopped and it didn't continue until after the Civil War with marble from the same Maryland quarries but of a different stratum and of a slightly different shade. At its completion, it was the world's tallest structure. It's still the tallest in D.C.

15th St. and Constitution Ave. NW.
Metro: Smithsonian

 Free; $2 service and handling
fee for advance tickets

Daily 9–5

202/426–6841; advance tickets
www.recreation.gov or 877/444–6777

5 and up

Each of the four sides has two viewing stations, and every other station is equipped with a step. Small children may think Washington looks like Legoland. Older children may enjoy trying to find Washington's landmarks. (A street map, available in the gift shop, is helpful for this.) On a very clear day, you can see Shenandoah National Park to the west and the stadium where the Washington Redskins play to the east.

When you're ready to land, descend one flight of stairs to the elevator. This level also houses a small bookshop that carries a modest selection of children's books. After being up in the monument, take a good look at the top of the monument from the ground. Unlike a pencil lead (made of graphite), the monument is topped with a 7½-pound piece of aluminum, a very expensive metal in 1884, when the monument was completed.

If you like this sight you may also like Mount Vernon (#41).

MAKE THE MOST OF YOUR TIME Judging by the crowds, it seems there are as many people who want to look down on the Washington action literally as there are those who look down on it figuratively. If you don't want to wait in line, head to Washington National Cathedral's Pilgrim Observation Gallery (*see* #5) or the Old Post Office (100 Pennsylvania Ave., at 12th St. NW, tel. 202/606–8691).

EATS FOR KIDS
A **refreshment stand** sells ice cream in summer and hot chocolate in winter, and sandwiches year-round. For some down-to-earth good food, *see* the restaurants listed for the United States Holocaust Memorial Museum (#10) and National Museum of American History (#30).

WASHINGTON NATIONAL CATHEDRAL

5

Boys and girls go Gothic at this, the sixth-largest cathedral in the world. Like its 14th-century counterparts, the National Cathedral (officially Washington's Cathedral Church of St. Peter and St. Paul) has flying buttresses and 100-foot vaulted ceilings that were built stone by stone. Fanciful gargoyles adorn the outside of the building. Inside, a stained-glass window with an encapsulated moon rock celebrates the *Apollo 11* space flight, and statues of George Washington and Abraham Lincoln stand as tributes.

The flags and seals for all 50 states can be found in the cathedral. Kids like counting the pennies in the floor of Lincoln Bay; or if you have a lot of time, see how far you get counting the pieces of stained glass that make up the West Rose window. There are more than 10,500!

Also of interest to young and old, the Pilgrim Observation Gallery provides a panoramic view of Washington. A charming children's chapel tantalizes the imagination with depictions of real and imaginary animals. Kneelers depict the story of Noah's ark.

MAKE THE MOST OF YOUR TIME While the cathedral is a cool place for kids, it's still a house of worship, so encourage children to be as quiet as, well, church mice, in the main church and chapels. If they need to let off steam, take them to the Bishop's Garden, ideal for hide-and-seek.

EATS FOR KIDS The only place to get something to eat on the cathedral grounds is the **museum shop** (tel. 202/537–6267), which has sandwiches and yogurt in a self-serve refrigerator. The cathedral is surrounded by green gardens that are great for a picnic, however. A few blocks north you can find **Cactus Cantina** (3300 Wisconsin Ave. NW, tel. 202/686–7222), a lively Mexican restaurant where President George W. Bush and Laura Bush dined, **Cafe Deluxe** (3228 Wisconsin Ave. NW, tel. 202/686–2233), which includes a three-vegetable entrée among its children's offerings, and **2 Amys** (3715 Macomb St., tel. 202/885–5700) known as the best gourmet pizza place in the city.

Massachusetts and Wisconsin Aves. NW

 Free; most children's programs $6

 202/537-6200, 202/537-2934 Family Programs; www.nationalcathedral.org

Memorial Day–Labor Day, M–F 10–7:45, Sa–Su 10–4; early Sept–late May, daily 10–5:30; Family Programs Sa 10–2

4 and up, Medieval Workshops 5 and up

Aside from seeing the cathedral itself, however, there are lots of other activities for kids. At the Gargoyle's Den (Saturdays 10–2), your children can create a clay gargoyle, carve limestone, piece together a stained-glass window, and make a brass rubbing while learning about the cathedral's construction and arts. You can drop in but workshops are not drop-off affairs: those under 12 must be accompanied by an adult. Be sure to check out the maze in the Bishop's Garden and the exotic bug-eating plants in the greenhouse.

On Family Saturdays, children 4–8 explore the nooks and crannies of the cathedral before making such topical crafts that change with the season. Sometimes children dye Easter eggs, arrange fresh flowers, make gingerbread cathedrals, or create mosaics with glass tiles.

If you like this sight, you may also like the United States Capitol (#11).

KEEP IN MIND At the east side of St. Peter's tower, almost at the top, is a stone grotesque of Darth Vader, a model of which is in the Medieval Workshop. A 13-year-old boy won a contest to design a decorative sculpture for the cathedral. Bring binoculars. They make Vader—and a lot of the other gargoyles—easier to spot.

4

Baseball fans have a lot to cheer about in D.C. In 2005, baseball returned to the District after a 33-year break, but it was played in an antiquated arena built in 1961 for football and baseball. In 2008, fans will consume peanuts and Cracker Jack in a brand new stadium built with attendees, players, and the environment in mind.

Despite its long hiatus, professional baseball enjoys a long and rich history in our nation's capital that extends back to the late 19th century. The very first professional team in D.C. was the Olympic Baseball Club of Washington in 1871. A team called Capital Cities from the League of Colored Baseball Clubs arrived in 1887. There was a huge African-American following of the game in the District. From the late 1930s through World War II, the Homestead Grays, perhaps the greatest Negro League team ever, ran the bases here.

The National's team colors are red, white, and blue with a touch of gold, but you can see fans sporting pink and purple caps as well. The team's mascot named Screech predictably

KEEP IN MIND Washington ,D.C., is also a mecca for youth soccer. If your kids get a kick out of this international sport, consider cheering on the D.C. United Soccer team (202/587–5000; www.dcunited.com), which plays at nearby RFK Stadium. One of 15 MLS (Major League Soccer) teams in the country, D.C. United has won more major national and international championships than any other U.S. team in history. Plays are called in both English and Spanish. Arrive early on weekends to participate in free speed kicks, dribbling contests, and other activities just for kids outside the stadium.

1500 S. Capitol St. SE. Metro: Navy Yard

 About $30

 Early-Apr–Oct. Gates open
1½ hr before game time

📞 202/675-6287; www.nationals.com

🛒 4 and up

is an eagle, but some folks think he looks more like a chicken! Screech greets fans in the stands and in the concourse of the stadium.

The Nationals, unofficially nicknamed the Nats, are also represented by a group of young adults called the Nat Pack that revs up the crowd and helps give away goodies that kids love—T-shirts, pizzas, and magnets. On Sunday after the game, kids take to the field for the diamond dash.

You can root for more than the Nats in this political town. Ten-foot tall caricatures of the presidents on Mount Rushmore take to the field in the middle of the fourth inning. Who will win? Washington, Jefferson, Lincoln, or Teddy Roosevelt? Find out at the game.

If you like this experience you may also like Bowie Baysox Baseball (#66).

MAKE THE MOST OF YOUR TIME The new stadium
is six quick Metro stops from the Smithsonian. The Metro is quick, easy, and preferable for most fans. Despite the crowds, it's far easier than catching the subway after the July 4 fireworks!

EATS FOR KIDS
You can munch on classic ballpark fare hot dogs, chicken tenders, and peanuts, but you can also order Chinese and Chesapeake Bay cuisine. Egg rolls or crab cakes anyone?

WHEATON REGIONAL PARK

All aboard! A little red replica of an 1863 train chugs along on 10-minute tours through the woods at this park within 10 mi of D.C. But there's more for children here than just choo-choo rides.

Youngsters can whiz around on a carousel, ride a life-size statue of a camel, or peer over the turrets of a castle in a sandbox that can accommodate a whole class of kids. The playground is packed with bouncing wooden bridges, ladders, swings, mazes, wooden jeeps with bright plastic steering wheels, and straight and spiral slides in all sizes—from less than 6 feet long to more than 60 feet long.

Facilities for sports lovers include hiking trails, an ice rink, tennis courts, baseball fields, and basketball courts. The Brookside Nature Center offers dozens of free and low-cost nature programs throughout the year, including hikes, puppet shows, workshops, and summer camps, but even without a special program, the nature center is a fun place to visit.

EATS FOR KIDS
Picnic tables are scattered throughout the park. If you're planning for a crowd, consider renting a picnic shelter (tel. 301/495–2525; www.parkpermits.org), where you're guaranteed a dry place to eat, rain or shine. **Westfield Wheaton** (11160 Viers Mill Rd., tel. 301/946–3200), about 3 mi away, has a food court.

MAKE THE MOST OF YOUR TIME
If you're closer to the Potomac, you might prefer the 528-acre Cabin John Regional Park (7400 Tuckerman Lane, Rockville, MD, tel. 301/299–0024). Your child can swing, slide, and climb on playground equipment or watch the Bethesda Big Train baseball team (tel. 301/983–1006; www.bigtrain.org) play in a summer league. Facilities here also include a train replica that takes children through the forest and alongside the playground, where kids often wave to the train passengers. Feed trash to the talking pig near the train station.

2000 Shorefield Rd., Wheaton, MD; Brookside nature center 1400 Glenallan Ave.; Brookside Gardens 1800 Glenallan Ave.

301/942-6703, 301/946-9071 nature center, 301/962-1400 gardens; www.montgomeryparks.org; www.brooksidenature.org; www.brooksidegardens.org

Free; some attractions charge

Daily sunrise-sunset; some attractions seasonal

6 months and up

Kids can check out live snakes, fish, and turtles; play nature games on the computer; and put puzzles together.

Next to the nature center is Brookside Gardens, where formal seasonal displays of bulbs, annuals, and perennials and a sprawling azalea garden flourish outside and seasonal displays and exotic tropicals blossom inside. Butterflies from North America and Costa Rica roam freely indoors at the Wings of Fancy exhibit from early May through mid-September. The garden's annual Children's Day held on the third or fourth Saturday in September, features activities, crafts, and games.

If you like this sight you may also like the United States National Arboretum (#9).

KEEP IN MIND You won't see Santa or a menorah at Brookside's Garden of Lights but you will see bears, owls, squirrels, cherry trees, and black-eyed Susans—all lit up brighter than stars to enchant children of all ages and all faiths. My family's not the only one that makes this a holiday tradition. For a decent parking space on weekends, be sure to arrive early.

WHITE HOUSE AND VISITOR CENTER

It's extraordinary and fortunate that America's most famous house is still open to visitors.

You can see the place that President Dwight Eisenhower called "a living story of past pioneering, struggles, wars, innovations, and a growing America," but it takes advance planning: You can only tour with a group, you'll need to gather a group of 10 or more, and you must make arrangements to tour through a member of Congress. To visit in January, a month might be sufficient notice, but to visit in spring or summer you'll need to request possible dates about six months in advance.

Tours last about 20–25 minutes and take you through the East Room (where Teddy Roosevelt allowed his children to ride a pony and where one of Abraham Lincoln's sons rode a goat through a reception), the Green Room, the Blue Room, the Red Room, and the State Dining Room (where Bill Clinton's daughter Chelsea hosted pizza parties).

MAKE THE MOST OF YOUR TIME Take a White House Un-Tour, an unofficial walking tour about the presidential mansion, and learn some official but off-the-wall fun facts, such as how many buckets of paint it takes to coat the White House. Kids can even "become" presidents and learn about changes—good or bad—they made to the Executive Mansion. Meet at 10 AM on Saturday and Sunday (Memorial Day–Labor Day) at the McPherson Square Metrorail Station, "White House" exit (tel. 202/484-1565; www.washingtonwalks.com; $10 adults, $5 kids 12 and under, younger than 3 free).

1600 Pennsylvania Ave. NW;
Visitor Center, 1450 Pennsylvania Ave. NW.
Metro: Federal Triangle

 Free

T–Sa 7:30–12:30 (groups only; tours
may be canceled without notice);
Visitor Center daily 7:30–4

202/456–7041 recording, 202/208–1631 voice;
www.whitehouse.gov; www.nps.gov/whho

 5 and up

Fortunately there's another place to learn about our country's most famous house without having to harass your congress member—through its visitor center, where a video tour of the house continually plays and you can see photos. Challenge your child to find the gingerbread house, the pet pony named Macaroni, and the family prankster who ate all the strawberries intended for a state dinner.

Just as if you were touring the actual White House, you can't bring in any food or drink, even water, with you. But unlike the president's place, the visitor center has room to roam and rest (seats and benches), as well as restrooms and water fountains, which aren't available on the White House tour.

If you like this sight you may also like the U.S. Capitol (#11).

KEEP IN MIND
The last time I toured the White House in January 2007, my friend Cheryl was supposed to go with our group, but we never caught up with her. Turns out she not only took the tour, she dropped in on an old friend of hers who works at the White House. So while we worried, Cheryl and her son Charlie were enjoying presidential M&Ms! Of course, the candies were red, white, and blue.

EATS FOR KIDS At **Old Ebbitt Grill** (675 15th St. NW, tel. 202/347–4800), a Washington tradition since 1856, parents like the homemade pasta, and children like the choices on the kids' menu including grilled cheese and hot dogs. But if the idea of spending $6 for a kids' meal makes you cringe, try the food hall in the **Shops** (National Place, F and G Sts. between 13th and 14th Sts. NW, tel. 202/662–1200) for everything from greasy fries to gourmet salads at more reasonable prices.

WOLF TRAP NATIONAL PARK
FOR THE PERFORMING ARTS

Over a stream and through the woods, you can find a clearing with benches and a stage where the National Park Service sponsors Theatre-in-the-Woods for at least seven weeks every summer. Though this venue is most often associated with adult concerts, as many as 800 people per performance come here to see professional children's performers, such as jugglers, musicians, clowns, storytellers, and puppeteers.

Afterward, romping through the park is encouraged. Children (and parents) roll down the grassy hill and picnic in the meadow under shady trees. Sometimes park rangers give impromptu nature tours after the performances. Rangers may point out Virginia's state tree (the dogwood) and bird (the cardinal). They may also talk about how the bark and roots of the sassafras tree were used not only to make perfume, soap, and medicine, but also to flavor root beer.

For one weekend in September, Wolf Trap hosts the International Children's Festival, which

KEEP IN MIND If you want to come back and see a performance at night, you'll have more than 100 to choose from between the outdoor Filene Center and the indoor Barns at Wolf Trap. Just be aware that everyone, even babes in arms, must have a ticket for performances.

MAKE THE MOST OF YOUR TIME Sometimes shows sell out so if your child really wants to see a certain performance or you want to introduce your child to an art (opera, for example), pick up tickets in advance at the Filene Center or call Ticket.com (tel. 703/218–6500). On Tuesday, Thursday, and Saturday after the 10 AM shows, performers stay for about 40 minutes to teach workshops for children 5 and up. Groups of about 35 kids gain insight into the performing arts, learning puppetry, proper clown etiquette, simple ballet techniques, or mime moves. Reservations are a must for the free workshops.

features performers, crafts, and music from other countries. Many of the entertainers are children, yet previous guests have included clowns from Ringling Brothers and Barnum & Bailey's circus, and Bob McGrath ("Bob" on *Sesame Street*) and his big yellow pal. Three stages—the Theatre-in-the-Woods, the Meadow Pavilion, and the Filene Center (a covered amphitheater)—feature entertainment from puppet shows to dances. Kids who want their faces or wrists painted can choose from more than the usual animal or flower—they can select a flag from one of the countries celebrated or a U.S. flag. One of the most popular festival areas is the Arts/Technology Pavilion. In the past, kids have designed roller coasters on computers, interacted with a robot, and boogied for video cameras.

Everything except food is included in the price. If it rains, everything moves to tents and the Filene Center but this doesn't dampen spirits too much.

If you like this sight you may also like Glen Echo Park (#51).

EATS FOR KIDS No food or drink (except water) is permitted in the theater, because of bees and animals that might want to nibble your lunch. If you bring food, you'll have to keep it securely wrapped in a squirrel-proof container (think hard plastic instead of paper) during the show. For evening performances at Wolf Trap, whether you bring your own food or buy from their **vendors**, you're welcome to stretch out on the lawn.

CLASSIC GAMES

"I SEE SOMETHING YOU DON'T SEE AND IT IS BLUE." Stuck for a way to get your youngsters to settle down in a museum? Sit them down on a bench in the middle of a room and play this vintage favorite. The leader gives just one clue—the color—and everybody guesses away.

"I'M GOING TO THE GROCERY..." The first player begins, "I'm going to the grocery and I'm going to buy... " and finishes the sentence with the name of an object, found in grocery stores, that begins with the letter "A." The second player repeats what the first player has said, and adds the name of another item that starts with "B." The third player repeats everything that has been said so far and adds something that begins with "C" and so on through the alphabet. Anyone who skips or misremembers an item is out (or decide up front that you'll give hints to all who need 'em). You can modify the theme depending on where you're going that day, as "I'm going to X and I'm going to see..."

FAMILY ARK Noah had his ark—here's your chance to build your own. It's easy: Just start naming animals and work your way through the alphabet, from antelope to zebra.

PLAY WHILE YOU WAIT

NOT THE GOOFY GAME Have one child name a category. (Some ideas: first names, last names, animals, countries, friends, feelings, foods, hot or cold things, clothing.) Then take turns naming things that fall into that category. You're out if you name something that doesn't belong in the category—or if you can't think of another item to name. When only one person remains, start again. Choose categories depending on where you're going or where you've been—historic topics if you've seen a historic sight, animal topics before or after the zoo, upside-down things if you've been to the circus, and so on. Make the game harder by choosing category items in A-B-C order.

DRUTHERS How do your kids really feel about things? Just ask. "Would you rather eat worms or hamburgers? Hamburgers or candy?" Choose serious and silly topics—and have fun!

BUILD A STORY "Once upon a time there lived..." Finish the sentence and ask the rest of your family, one at a time, to add another sentence or two. Bring a tape recorder along to record the narrative—and you can enjoy your creation again and again.

GOOD TIMES GALORE

WIGGLE & GIGGLE Give your kids a chance to stick out their tongues at you. Start by making a face, then have the next person imitate you and add a gesture of his own—snapping fingers, winking, clapping, sneezing, or the like. The next person mimics the first two and adds a third gesture, and so on.

JUNIOR OPERA During a designated period of time, have your kids sing everything they want to say.

THE QUIET GAME Need a good giggle—or a moment of calm to figure out your route? The driver sets a time limit and everybody must be silent. The last person to make a sound wins.

BEST BETS

BEST IN TOWN
International Spy Museum
Mount Vernon
National Air and Space Museum
National Museum of American History
National Zoo

BEST OUTDOORS
Wheaton Regional Park (gardens and nature center)

WACKIEST
D.C. Ducks

GROSSEST
National Museum of Health and Medicine

BEST CULTURAL ACTIVITY
National Gallery of Art and Sculpture Garden

BEST MUSEUM
National Museum of Natural History

SOMETHING FOR EVERYONE

ART ATTACK
Corcoran Gallery of Art, **59**
Hirshhorn Museum and Sculpture Garden, **48**
National Gallery of Art and Sculpture Garden, **33**
National Museum of African Art, **31**
National Museum of Women in the Arts, **26**
Phillips Collection, **20**
Sackler Gallery/Freer Gallery of Art, **17**
Smithsonian American Art Museum and the National Portrait Gallery, **15**

CULTURE CLUB
National Museum of African Art, **31**
Sackler Gallery/Freer Gallery of Art, **17**

FARMS AND ANIMALS
Claude Moore Colonial Farm at Turkey Run, **61**
National Aquarium, **37**
National Zoo, **24**
Oxon Cove Park, **22**
Patuxent National Wildlife Visitor Center, **21**
Rock Creek Park, **19**

GOOD SPORTS
Bowie Baysox Baseball, **66**
Mystics Basketball, **40**
Washington Nationals, **4**
Wheaton Regional Park, **3**

HISTORIC HOUSES
Children's Museum of Rose Hill Manor Park, **62**
Frederick Douglass National Historic Site, **52**
Glen Echo Park, **51**
Mount Vernon, **41**
Sully Historic Site, **14**
White House and Visitor Center, **2**

LOST IN SPACE
College Park Aviation Museum, **60**
Goddard Space Flight Center, **50**
National Air and Space Museum, **39**
National Air and Space Museum's Steven F. Udvar-Hazy Center, **38**

ALL AROUND TOWN

MANY THANKS

This book is dedicated with appreciation to the Smithsonian Institution employees and volunteers, the National Park Service rangers, and all the museum guides, naturalists, and docents who make Washington such an enriching environment for children. On a personal note: For helping me to witness Washington's wonders through the eyes of children, I am grateful to my sons, Norman and Tim, and their nine cousins, Anastasia, Brady, Diana, Eddie, Erin, Kate, Mary, Matthew, and Owen.

—Kathryn McKay

the end.